MINECRAFT

First published in Great Britain 2023 by Farshore
An imprint of HarperCollins*Publishers*
1 London Bridge Street, London SE1 9GF
www.farshore.co.uk

HarperCollins*Publishers*
Macken House,
39/40 Mayor Street Upper,
Dublin 1
D01 C9W8

Special thanks to Sherin Kwan, Alex Wiltshire, Jay Castello and Kelsey Ranallo.

ISBN 978 0 00 860850 7
Printed in Italy
1

ONLINE SAFETY FOR YOUNGER FANS

Spending time online is great fun! Here are a few simple rules to help younger fans stay safe and keep the internet a great place to spend time:

- Never give out your real name – don't use it as your username.
- Never give out any of your personal details.
- Never tell anybody which school you go to or how old you are.
- Never tell anybody your password except a parent or a guardian.
- Be aware that you must be 13 or over to create an account on many sites. Always check the site policy and ask a parent or guardian for permission before registering.
- Always tell a parent or guardian if something is worrying you.

Stay safe online. Any website addresses listed in this book are correct at the time of going to print. However, Farshore is not responsible for content hosted by third parties. Please be aware that online content can be subject to change and websites can contain content that is unsuitable for children. We advise that all children are supervised when using the internet.

Stay safe online. Farshore is not responsible for content hosted by third parties.
All information and stats are based on Minecraft: Bedrock Edition.

MIX
Paper | Supporting responsible forestry
FSC™ C007454
www.fsc.org

This book is produced from independently certified FSC™ paper to ensure responsible forest management.

For more information visit: www.harpercollins.co.uk/green

MINECRAFT

EXPLORER'S HANDBOOK

MOJANG STUDIOS

CONTENTS

YOUR JOURNEY BEGINS

TEMPERATE LANDSCAPES

HOT LANDSCAPES

COLD LANDSCAPES

AQUATIC LANDSCAPES

UNDERGROUND LANDSCAPES

THE NETHER

THE END

WELCOME TO THE MINECRAFT EXPLORER'S HANDBOOK!

The world of Minecraft is a vast and varied place. You can tame horses on grassy plains and trek through dense jungles to spot parrots and pandas. Or you can discover mysterious pyramids in rolling desert sands and scale eerie ice spikes to look out over frozen seas.

And don't forget about the Nether and the End! They may be dangerous, but rare resources and exciting adventures await the brave explorer who knows how to survive in them.

With the help of this book, you'll become that explorer. Whether you're looking to learn all there is to know about climbing the tallest mountains or you'd prefer to dive to the bottom of a squid-filled ocean, it will be your guide to every biome, detailing what you'll find in them and what challenges lie ahead.

Whether your Minecraft journey is just getting started or you're a seasoned adventurer, there's always something new to see, just beyond that hill ...

SO LET'S GET EXPLORING!

- MOJANG STUDIOS

1

YOUR ADVENTURE BEGINS

Every journey has a beginning and, by opening this handbook, you have shown a desire to start yours. While you will be tempted to jump straight into the action, it is essential to be well prepared. Let's start by looking at the basic skills you will need to survive as an Overworld explorer.

HOME SWEET HOME

COLLECT

Your first action should be to look for nearby trees and gather some wood from their trunks. Open your crafting menu and turn these into planks to create a crafting table.

Crafting table recipe

CRAFT

Using the supplies of wood you collected, craft more planks and then some sticks. Now, you'll be able to create some tools, such as a wooden pickaxe. Use it to go and mine some cobblestone and then use that to craft some stone tools.

Wooden pickaxe recipe

Oak door recipe

BUILD

Night will soon arrive and hostile mobs with it. Stay safe by using cobblestone blocks to build a small base with a flat roof. It can be as small as 4x5 blocks. Craft a wooden door so you can go in and out, but hostile mobs cannot.

TOP TIP

It is tempting to gather only the amount of resources that you need immediately. But you can store most resources in stacks of 64 – it's always good to have extra!

You've spawned! Welcome to the Overworld. There's so much to see that you'll want to start exploring straight away, but there is some essential preparation to take care of first. The land is full of excitement, but when nighttime comes, it will bring danger with it.

ESSENTIAL ITEMS

WEAPONS

As beautiful as the Overworld is, there are threats that you will need to defend yourself against. Some can be outsmarted but others will require weapons, such as a sword or a bow.

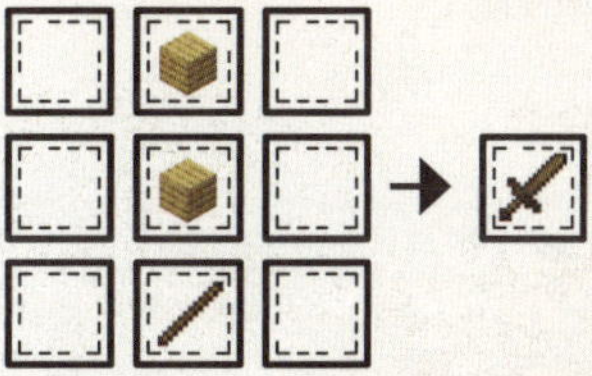

Wooden sword recipe

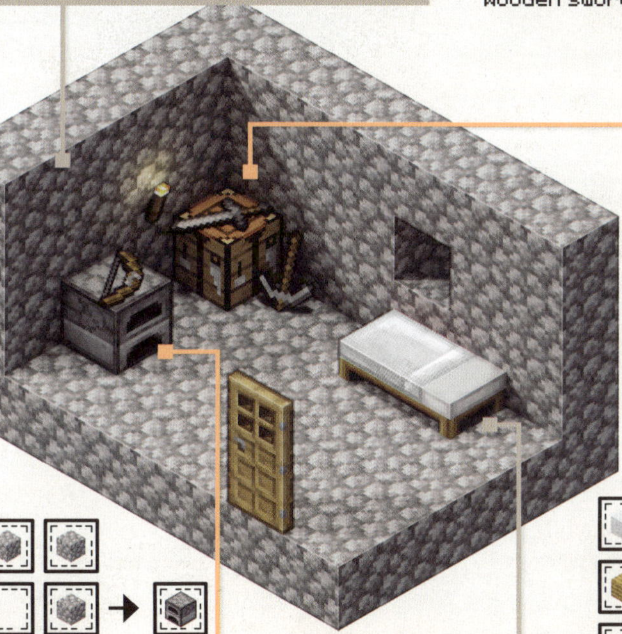

TOOLS

Stone tools may last longer than those made of wood, but they will also wear out and need replacing. It's a good idea to craft extras and carry them in your inventory, so you aren't caught out.

Furnace recipe

Bed recipe

FOOD

You can craft a furnace using 8 blocks of cobblestone. This utility block can be used to cook food to replenish your hunger, such as steak or mutton. It can also smelt ores to make more durable weapons and tools.

BED

A bed doesn't only allow you to sleep through the night, it will also act as your spawn point in the game. If any tragedy befalls you, this is the location where you will respawn. To craft one, you will need wooden planks and wool from a sheep.

REWARDS AND DANGERS

REWARDS

DIAMOND

With an iron pickaxe or stronger, you can mine diamond ore and it will drop a single diamond. These can be used to craft high-tier armour and equipment, which offer increased durability and greater damage.

IRON

Iron ore can be found underground. Breaking it will drop raw iron, which you can smelt in a furnace to get iron ingots. This crafting ingredient is useful for upgrading your weapons and armour.

GOLD

If you're using an iron pickaxe or stronger, you will be able to break valuable ores, such as gold. Crafting with gold offers faster mining speed and better enchantability, but less durability and it can't mine all blocks.

TOP TIP

Defeating mobs can result in them dropping items or resources. For example, skeletons often drop arrows and zombies may drop weapons. Many animals will also drop meat that can be cooked and eaten to keep your hunger levels healthy.

There's a whole world waiting to be explored and it's full of unique locations and useful resources to discover. Around every corner of each cave could be valuable rewards, but there could also be harmful dangers lurking just out of sight ...

DANGERS

HOSTILE MOBS

Hostile mobs are aggressive and will attack you if you are within their detection range. Throughout this Handbook, we will look at some ways to stay safe on your travels.

LAVA

You will find lava across the Overworld. Its warm glow might be appealing, but don't get too close ... the damage it inflicts could be fatal.

WATER

The Overworld is home to vast oceans and winding rivers. You can only hold your breath for 15 seconds, so swim with caution.

POWDER SNOW

In extremely cold locations, you might come across powder snow. If you're not prepared, you will fall into it, move slowly and begin to suffer from harmful freeze damage.

HEIGHTS

It's fun to climb mountains. The views from high locations are rewarding, but the potential fall can make them extra perilous. Falling from 23 blocks or higher can be fatal.

ARMOUR

PROTECTION

Wearing armour can be the difference between sudden death or living to tell the tale. It enables you to take more damage and will decrease how quickly your health points go down. Armour can be enchanted in many ways and can help you survive in freezing conditions, or even journey underwater for longer periods.

EARLY GAME ARMOUR

You should try to wear armour as soon as possible. Leather can be gathered from defeated cows and used to craft leather armour, which offers basic defence and has its own benefits, such as protection from freezing.

TOP TIP

Taking damage will decrease the condition of your armour. If it breaks when you're lost in a deep cave network, or in the Nether, you could be in real trouble. Always try to keep some spare armour in your inventory, to equip when you need it most.

ADVANCED MATERIALS

As you become a more experienced explorer who has travelled to many biomes and dimensions, you will gather different materials that can be used to increase the effectiveness of your armour.

Diamond and netherite are hard to find, but offer the toughest protection.

From your very first steps into the unknown, the many dangers of the Overworld will be present. Preparation is an essential element of an explorer's life, and being ready to protect yourself from attacks should be one of your first considerations.

HELMET

Any helmet is used in the head slot on your inventory screen. They can give you up to three armour points and can even be enchanted to offer additional safety or abilities. Fire Protection is particularly useful if you're exploring the Nether.

CHESTPLATE

The mighty chestplate is worn in the torso slot and offers more armour points than any other item. You can enchant it in various ways, such as Projectile Protection – perfect for surviving surprise ranged attacks.

LEGGINGS

Your lower-body slot is where you can equip leggings. They don't offer as much protection as a chestplate, but you can still increase their durability with an Unbreaking enchantment.

BOOTS

Boots offer the least protection, but they will complete your look and are not without their uses. Using the Depth Strider enchantment will increase your speed underwater, while basic leather boots will protect you from taking freeze damage from powder snow.

FOOD AND SUPPLIES

FOOD

Hunger is affected by everything you do in Minecraft. It can have a huge impact on your ability to survive an adventure, so it's important to be prepared before setting off. Make the most of exploring above ground, where food options are usually plentiful.

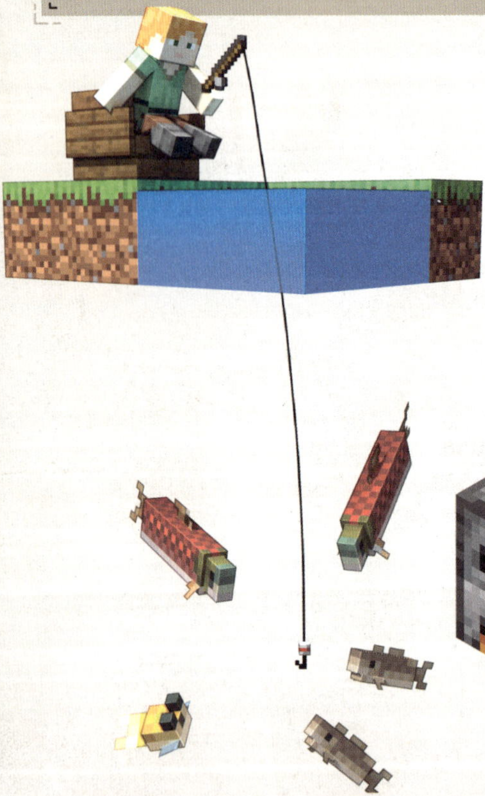

RAW MEAT		COOKED MEAT	
RAW BEEF	3	COOKED BEEF	8
RAW PORKCHOP	3	COOKED PORKCHOP	8
RAW CHICKEN	2	COOKED CHICKEN	6
RAW MUTTON	2	COOKED MUTTON	6
RAW RABBIT	3	COOKED RABBIT	5

COOKING

When you defeat animals, they will drop raw meat or fish (cooked if defeated with fire), which you can eat to restore hunger points. If raw, cook them in a furnace to maximise the hunger points you replenish.

RAW FISH		COOKED FISH	
RAW COD	2	COOKED COD	5
RAW SALMON	2	COOKED SALMON	6
TROPICAL FISH	1	TROPICAL FISH CAN'T BE COOKED	

TOP TIP

Vegetables can also be consumed to build up your hunger points. If you find any potatoes, carrots or beetroot then pick them up and keep them for later! Many crops also have alternative uses ...

While it's vitally important to have weapons, tools and armour in your inventory, you should also reserve space for food and supplies. Knowing what to take with you on your travels can avoid inconvenient situations, such as running out of food in the desert or deep underground.

SUPPLIES

Your inventory has space for 4 armour slots, an off-hand slot, 27 storage slots and 9 hotbar slots that will show up on your HUD. Most items can be stacked up to 64 of the same item in one slot, so always gather as many as you can and organise them efficiently.

TOP TIP

After spawning, some of the first items you craft will also be some of the most important. On long expeditions, the basics can often keep you safe.

BOAT

Crossing bodies of water can take time and subject you to several dangers. A boat can help on both counts and is simple to craft.

FURNACE

A furnace can cook food, smelt materials such as iron and gold, and create charcoal. You can use it anywhere if you have fuel.

TORCH

Torches are essential. Their light prevents mobs from spawning close to you – useful when mining, so you don't get ambushed.

WOOD

Wood is used for crafting weapons and many other items, such as torches, boats and beds. It is also a useful furnace fuel.

CHOOSE YOUR EQUIPMENT

WEAPONS

TYPES						
ATTACK STRENGTH	5	6	7	5	8	9
DURABILITY	60	132	251	33	1562	2032

SWORD

If you need a melee weapon, the sword delivers the most damage over time, so it's useful against mobs that can't be defeated with one swing. It can be crafted from a wooden stick and one of any six materials, from weak wood to tough netherite.

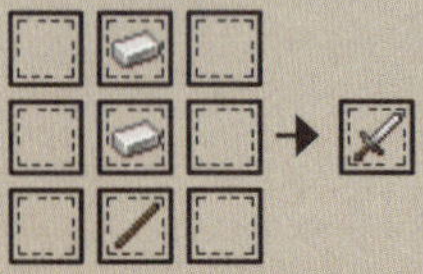

Iron sword recipe

TYPES						
ATTACK STRENGTH	4	5	6	4	7	8
DURABILITY	60	132	251	33	1562	2032

AXE

An axe is the quickest way to break any wooden blocks, such as logs and planks. Like the sword, its durability will be higher depending on what materials it's crafted from. It's also a handy weapon if you are caught without a sword, though it's not quite as strong.

Iron axe recipe

TYPES	
ATTACK STRENGTH	1-11
DURABILITY	384

BOW

The chosen weapon of skeletons everywhere, the bow is a ranged weapon, perfect for taking out any mobs you can't get too close to, such as creepers. You will need arrows to use a bow and the time to aim.

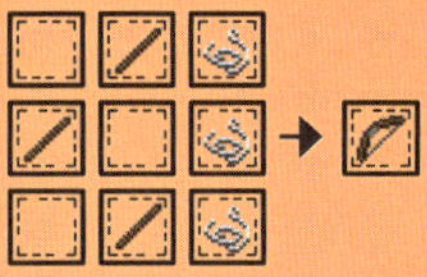

Bow recipe

TYPES	
ATTACK STRENGTH	9
DURABILITY	464

CROSSBOW

The crossbow requires more ingredients to craft than most weapons. They can shoot farther than a bow, so they increase range, but do take longer to load. They can launch firework rockets for explosive combat results.

Crossbow recipe

TYPES	
ATTACK STRENGTH	8-9
DURABILITY	250

TRIDENT

A trident is a powerful weapon for melee and ranged attacks. To get one, you'll need to defeat a drowned armed with a trident and, if you're lucky, they'll drop it.

Being properly equipped is the greatest secret to being a successful survivalist. In an ideal Overworld, you will be ready for any situation, be it farming or fighting. Let's look at the basic tools, how to craft them and when to use them.

TOOLS

TYPES						
ATTACK STRENGTH	3	4	5	3	6	7
DURABILITY	59	131	250	32	1561	2031

HOE

Hoes can be used to create farmland out of dirt blocks, grass blocks and dirt paths to make them suitable for planting crops. This is very useful if you'd like to create your own farm, especially because they can also be used to harvest most crops, as well.

Iron hoe recipe

TYPES						
ATTACK STRENGTH	3	4	5	3	6	7
DURABILITY	59	131	250	32	1561	2031

PICKAXE

There's a good chance you will find this to be the tool you use the most. It's the best tool for mining ores, stone blocks and metal-based blocks. It also doubles up as an effective melee weapon if you're caught in a pinch, but it's slower than a sword in a fight.

Iron pickaxe recipe

TYPES						
ATTACK STRENGTH	2	3	4	2	5	6
DURABILITY	59	131	250	32	1561	2031

SHOVEL

There will come a time when you need to dig through a bunch of dirt blocks to either mine or shape a landscape. There is no quicker way to do so than with a shovel. It can also be used to create dirt paths that make it easier to find your way to and from a destination.

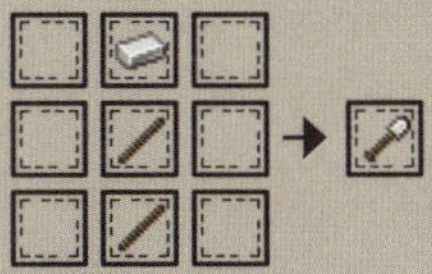

Iron shovel recipe

PLANNING YOUR ROUTES

COMPASS

It's all too easy to lose your way and struggle to find your way back to base. A compass will always point in the direction of your world's spawn point, making it easier to find your way back there.

LODESTONE

Using a compass on a lodestone will cause the compass needle to point to the lodestone instead of the world spawn point. These are crafted with netherite, found only in the Nether, so they are not easily craftable for new explorers.

WHERE SHOULD YOU GO?

Knowing where to go depends on your goals. Some are happy wandering until they stumble across something, but others like to search for specific locations. This book will help you choose an adventure to explore.

WHAT SHOULD YOU SEARCH FOR?

Your adventures depend on what you want to experience. Maybe you'd like to collect enough diamond ore to craft some new armour, or you might want to witness every mob in existence? The choice is yours ...

There's so much to do and see in Minecraft that it can be difficult to know where to begin. There are many biomes to discover, with resources, interesting inhabitants and unique structures that are just waiting to be explored. Let's take a look at some of the best ways you can reach them.

BY FOOT

You can cover huge distances by walking. Sprinting drains your hunger bar faster until you're too hungry to do it anymore.

HORSE

By taming a horse and equipping a saddle, you can use it to ride. It's a quick way to travel and offers improved jumping abilities.

DONKEY

Found wandering the plains, donkeys might be slower than horses, but they can carry a chest. Make sure you equip a saddle first.

MULE

The result of breeding a horse with a donkey, mules are faster than donkeys but slower than horses, and can carry chests.

CAMEL

Camels have the unique ability of stepping up 1.5 blocks (more than other rideable mobs), dashing across ravines and carrying two players at once.

TOP TIP

Horses, donkeys and mules (and pigs!) can be towed behind a boat using a lead. This means you can travel with your trusted steeds over water!

MAP MAKING

OBTAINING A MAP

You can craft a map using 8 paper (crafted from sugar cane). If you also use a compass (crafted from redstone dust and iron ingots), you'll be able to add location markers. You can add this later with a compass at an anvil, crafting table or cartography table.

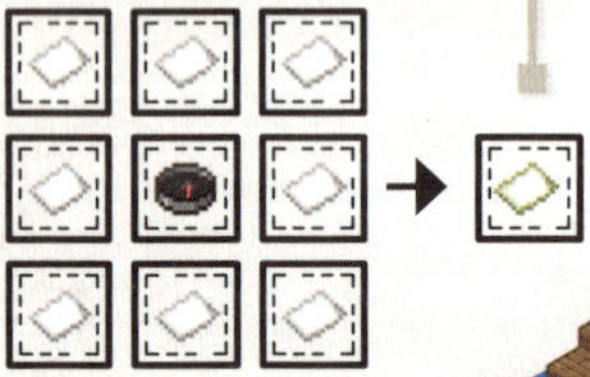

Map recipe

CARTOGRAPHY TABLE

You can find cartography tables inside cartographer houses in villages. They can be used to craft an empty map using just a single piece of paper. They also allow you to zoom in and out of maps to create larger recordings of your world, so you can locate any structures you've discovered, such as shipwrecks.

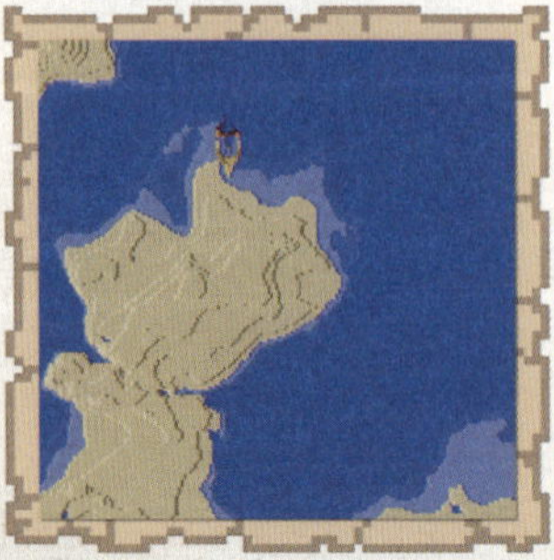

Sometimes, you might discover a structure but need to return to it later. By holding and using a map near it, you will mark its location, so you can easily find it again.

There's so much to explore that you might struggle to remember it all. The places you've been, the sights you've seen, the resources you didn't have inventory space for and promised you'd return to ... maps offer a way to keep track of all your travels and discoveries.

USING A MAP

When you are using it, a map will draw a top-down view of your surroundings and everywhere you travel. You can see your own position on the map and even mark points of interest or places to explore later, such as pillager outposts.

NETHER TRACKING

It is possible to use maps in the Nether, but with limited results. Terrain won't be mapped as you use it and your player marker will spin, making navigation difficult. However, marking waypoints with framed maps can still be useful.

MEET THE MOBS

CARTOGRAPHER VILLAGER

Most villagers seek to gain a profession, aside from nitwits. A cartographer will trade emeralds for a map, and later ocean explorer and woodland explorer maps. Look for them in any village.

2

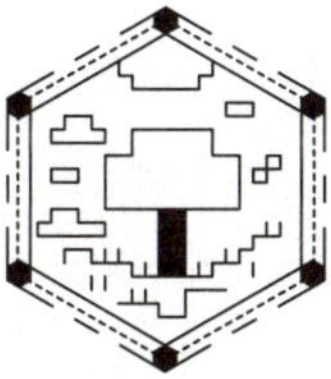

TEMPERATE LANDSCAPES

Here we go! It's time to venture out and there's no better place to begin than the following biomes. With their mild climates, you won't have to combat any freezing temperatures or intense heat, but you will find there is lots of fun to be had, much to be cautious about and even more to discover.

BIOMES: PLAINS

FLATLANDS

The plains are mostly grassy and flat with occasional flowers and clusters of trees, often found close to water. Because of this, they are an excellent place for beginner explorers to find their feet and discover how to survive.

USEFUL VIEWS

Don't be fooled by how flat plains are above ground. That just makes it easier to spot any cave openings, which can lead to vast networks of underground areas just waiting to be explored. Just make sure you're prepared before venturing below the surface.

As one of the most common biomes in the Overworld, plains will look familiar to most explorers. Their grasslands are often sparse and offer a good view of the surrounding areas, so many explorers choose to position their bases here. However, they are also full of things to discover!

SUNFLOWER PLAINS

This rarer variant of the plains is named after its sunflowers, which are found nowhere else in the Overworld. These colourful, golden-petalled flowers can make it feel like summer even in the middle of a thunderstorm.

TOP TIP

Sunflowers not only add a burst of colour to the Overworld, but they can be an explorer's best friend, too. If you're ever lost and without a compass, sunflowers always point to the east, which can help you navigate in the correct direction.

BUILD A BASE

Plains are a great location to build a base. They are often bordered by forests, giving you a good supply of wood. They are also home to many passive mobs, offering a constant supply of food. You might not want to tuck in to the rotten flesh of a zombie, though.

MEET THE MOBS

ZOMBIE

Although you will encounter zombies across many biomes, they are often witnessed on the plains – after dark, of course. You may hear their undead moans before you see them, but once they arrive, their melee attacks are capable of causing you serious damage, especially when they're in groups.

GENERATED STRUCTURES: VILLAGES

BUILDINGS

Positioned around a central meeting point, villages are made up of buildings that have different roles in the community. Some smaller houses contain beds and chests, while others offer services, such as a butcher shop or armourer's house.

VILLAGERS

This passive mob can be found in and around villages, going about their daily lives. They have jobs, interact with one another and will even trade with you. Just don't treat them poorly – they will retain memories about you and tell the other villagers.

TRADING

The trading system allows you to buy and sell items with villagers. You can only trade with villagers that have professions and will need emeralds and other items to use as currency. Simply walk up to a villager and interact with them to see their inventory and if they have anything that could be useful for your adventure.

There's nothing like the first moment you catch sight of a village. You can be exploring deep in the wild when suddenly a group of buildings comes into view. Embrace your inner curiosity, walk on in and you will find more than just a safe place for weary travellers ...

NIGHT NIGHT

If you need a safe place to sleep, there aren't many places better than a village. You can sleep in any bed that isn't currently occupied, and some structures also have a chest or two, containing items that you may find useful.

RAIDS

If you enter a village while you have the Bad Omen effect, you will trigger a raid and waves of attacks. If you stay to defend the village, you could get the Hero of the Village status effect, which discounts your trades with villagers.

ABANDONED VILLAGE

Also known as a zombie village, these are a ghostly sight to behold. Many structures will have fallen into a state of disrepair with areas covered in cobwebs. If you find one, proceed with extreme caution – zombie villagers dwell here.

MEET THE MOBS

IRON GOLEM

These large mobs are strong giants that will defend villagers. They patrol villages and will attack anyone or anything that causes trouble, including you. Their attacks involve swinging their arms up to fling enemies into the air. You can craft your own iron golem using 4 iron blocks and a pumpkin.

BIOMES: FORESTS

FLOWER FOREST

Flower forests have fewer trees than regular forests, with more open spaces that are covered in clusters of beautiful flowers. This makes them a good place to find if you are searching for dye, which can be used in decoration for colouring items and even sheep!

BIRCH FOREST

Thanks to the lighter colour of birch trees' trunks, these areas appear a bit brighter than other forests. While they may look similar, their old growth variation features taller trees, which tower as high as 14 blocks – meaning there is more wood to harvest there.

DARK FOREST

The many trees in dark forests block sunlight to create a darker environment for hostile mobs to spawn. Keep an eye out for giant mushrooms breaking up the canopy and dark oak trees – they are rare and can only be found in a few biomes.

One of the most common biomes to spawn in, many forests have a lot of similarities. It can be easy to stroll from one to another without realising, but get to know their subtle differences and you will be rewarded with knowing the different resources they offer and dangers they pose.

DANGERS

If you're a beginner, forests are a good place to practise, thanks to their lack of environmental dangers. That's not to say there are none, though. Dangerous mobs can hide for days in the shade of the trees.

RESOURCES

With their abundance of trees, forests are the best biomes for collecting wood for all of your crafting needs. You may even be lucky and find some apples hidden among the oak leaves, as well as other delights such as bees, flowers and many passive mobs hidden among the trees.

GET LOST

It can be quite easy to become lost when wandering in forests. If you lose your bearings, the density of the trees can make it hard to see which way you came from. Always remember, the sun rises in the east and sets in the west, but if you're still outside when it's setting, then you best start finding somewhere to spend the night.

MEET THE MOBS

WOLF

Wolves are a common sight in forests. Feed them with bones and they will soon be tame and follow you around, and possibly breed to create pups. This loyal mob is useful to have around as they will help defend you by attacking skeletons and their variants.

GENERATED STRUCTURES: WOODLAND MANSION

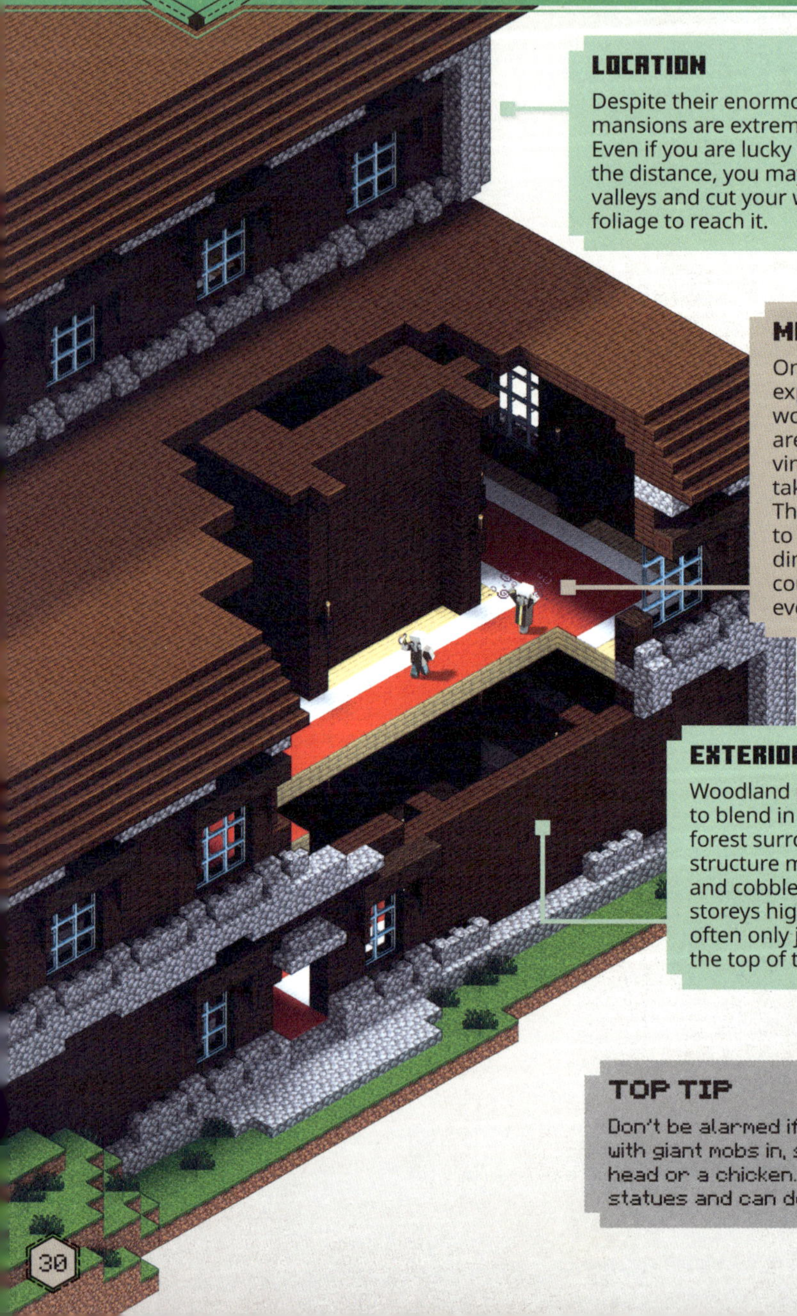

LOCATION

Despite their enormous size, woodland mansions are extremely hard to locate. Even if you are lucky enough to spot one in the distance, you may need to cross deep valleys and cut your way through thick foliage to reach it.

MOBS

Only the bravest explorers should enter a woodland mansion. They are home to evokers and vindicators, who don't take kindly to intruders. The hallways are a maze to navigate and are dimly lit, so hostile mobs could be lurking around every corner ...

EXTERIOR

Woodland mansions are built to blend in with their dark forest surroundings, with a structure made of dark wood and cobblestone. They are three storeys high and their roofs will often only just peek out above the top of the treeline.

TOP TIP

Don't be alarmed if you discover a room with giant mobs in, such as an illager head or a chicken. They are just statues and can do you no harm!

Only the most adventurous of explorers are likely to find a woodland mansion. They usually generate thousands of blocks from your spawn point, making them hard to find. They are also only found in dark forests, where survival becomes increasingly difficult the deeper you explore.

EXPLORER TIPS

CAPTIVE

Look out for prison cells. Nobody knows the history of these ghastly rooms, but vindicators can be found inside. You may also find allays – if you do, hand them an item and they will follow you.

FARM ROOM

Although every mansion is different, they will always contain farming rooms. From wheat to mushroom farms, these can provide useful ingredients to prepare your own food.

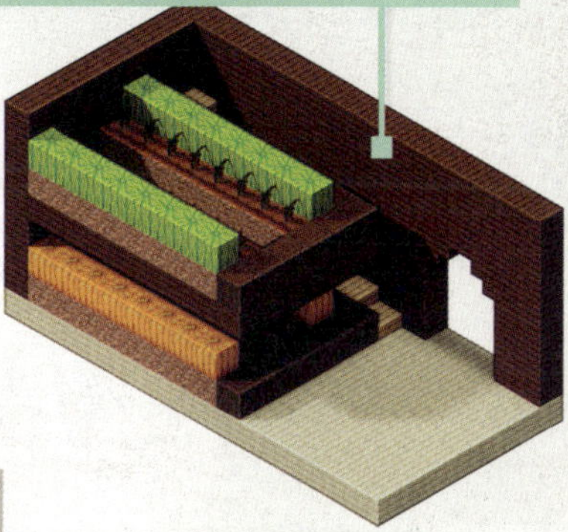

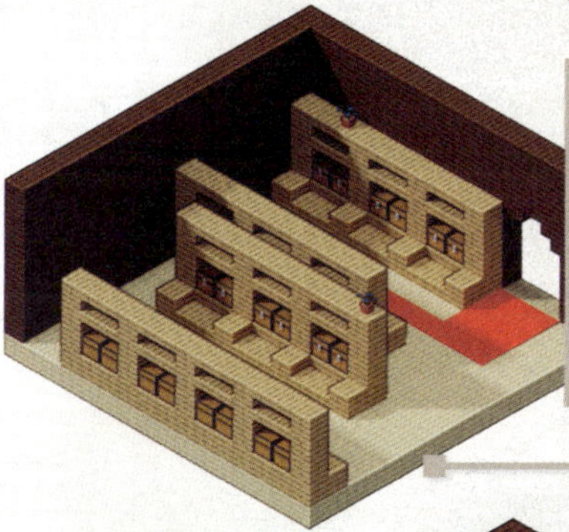

STORAGE ROOM

Entire rooms lined with chests? A just reward for making it into a woodland mansion. However, they're guarded by a vindicator, so you'll need to watch out!

SECRET ROOM

Woodland mansions sometimes have secret rooms. If you can find them, you could witness a fake End portal room, an obsidian room, or something else quite mysterious. What will you find?

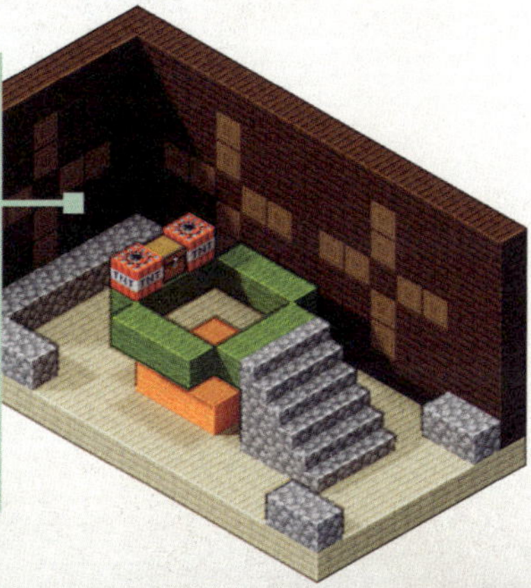

MEET THE MOBS

EVOKER

Evokers are hostile mobs that can cast spells, but you won't want to witness their magic. They can summon vexes to cause you harm and unleash a fang attack, which will cause fangs to come up from the ground and damage anyone in their path.

BIOMES: JUNGLES

Jungles are a visual treat for brave explorers. There is an abundance of tall and thick trees, making it is easy to get lost and even trapped when you're trying to escape hostile mobs.

JUNGLES

There's no mistaking a jungle. Its native trees are the tallest in the Overworld and the uneven terrain can make any journey feel like a maze that's hard to escape.

SPARSE JUNGLE

With its smaller trees, the sparse jungle is a much more convenient location for a base, with safer open spaces and room to build and farm.

BAMBOO JUNGLE

You'll likely witness a panda enjoying the bamboo here. The climate is more humid than other jungles, leading to a high chance of lush caves generating underneath.

MEET THE MOBS

PARROT

Found only in the jungles, this rare mob has real hidden talents. It is capable of imitating the sounds of hostile mobs that are within 20 block spaces of you and it can even sit on your shoulder!

FRIENDLY FACES

There are several friendly faces to be found in jungles. Pandas, parrots and ocelots all spawn almost exclusively in jungles and have different characteristics. A tamed ocelot can be kept on a lead, and will cause creepers to stay away from you.

GENERATED STRUCTURES: JUNGLE TEMPLE

Thanks to the dense foliage of their surroundings, jungle temples are incredibly difficult to locate. Their mossy cobblestone walls blend into the landscape, and much of their mystery lies below the surface ...

TRAPS

Even if you have cleared any hostile mobs lurking in their corridors, jungle temples are dangerous places. Be cautious of tripwire traps that can trigger arrow launchers.

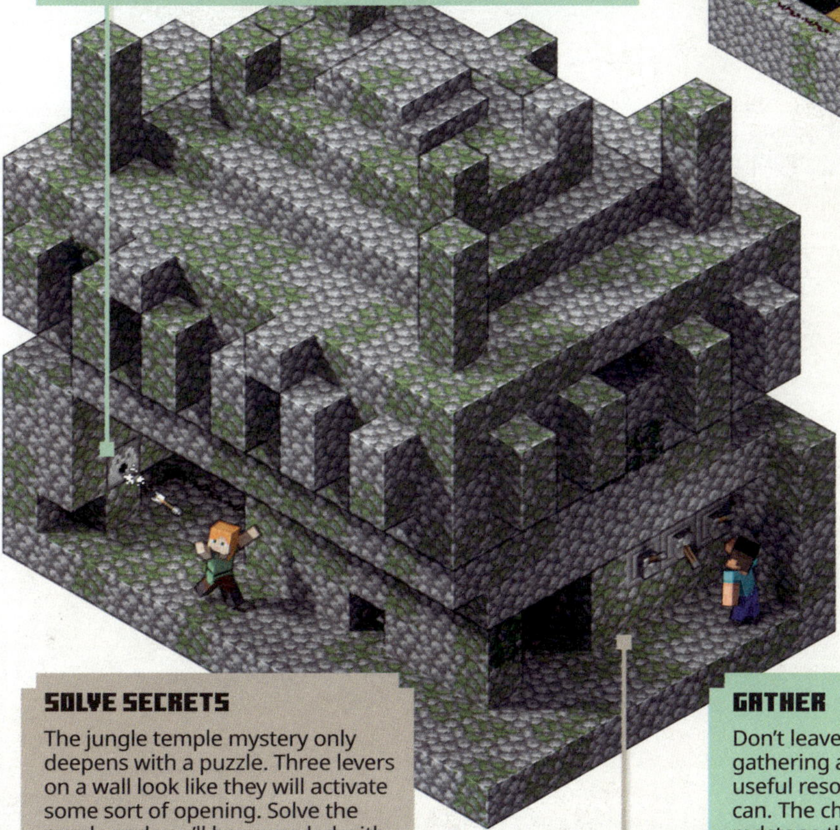

SOLVE SECRETS

The jungle temple mystery only deepens with a puzzle. Three levers on a wall look like they will activate some sort of opening. Solve the puzzle and you'll be rewarded with access to a secret room.

GATHER

Don't leave without gathering as many useful resources as you can. The chest trap uses redstone that you can help yourself to.

BIOMES:
CHERRY GROVE

You might not come across this uncommon biome very often, but it's impossible to mistake it when you do. They are named for their trees, which bring a cheery colour and falling blossom petals to the grassy landscape.

CHERRY TREES

The cherry grove's outstanding feature is the pale pink leaves of its cherry trees, which can only be found naturally here. However, you can gather cherry tree saplings to plant and enjoy their fluffy, pink appearance anywhere!

WOOD SET

You can break down cherry tree wood and take it as a souvenir of your travels. With its unique appearance, it can be used for exciting builds and accessories, such as a stunning pink hanging sign.

MEET THE MOBS

BEES

These cute neutral mobs live in nests and hover around during the day in search of flowers to pollinate to make honey. Just don't anger one, or all nearby bees will swarm together to attack you!

BIOMES: SWAMPS

In between the oak trees, vines and dead bushes, you will find much of a swamp biome is flooded with stagnant swamp waters. Listen for the croaking of frogs and you might witness these swamp dwellers' magnificent leap.

SWAMP HUT

These simple wooden structures hold sinister surprises within. The cackle of a witch should be the only warning you need as to what lies ahead of you. Defeat the witch and you may find a potion in their cauldron.

MEET THE MOBS

SLIME

Slime spawns more often during a full moon, so be alert for their bouncing sounds. If you think you've defeated one, be careful – it splits into smaller versions as it takes damage!

TOP TIP

When exploring warmer biomes, you may find yourself in a mangrove swamp. Do not spend time looking for a swamp hut in one of these, as these structures only generate in common swamps.

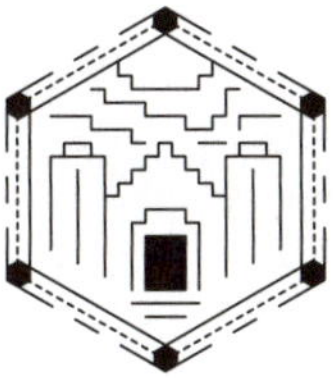

HOT LANDSCAPES

Although some hot biomes are scarce in resources and difficult to survive in, stocking up to explore them is worthwhile. Despite the difficulties of the dry and barren surface, these are biomes of unique beauty and home to several hidden riches, just waiting to be unearthed by explorers.

BIOMES: DESERTS

ON THE HORIZON

Thanks to its sandy surface and flat landscape, there's no such thing as a bad view of the desert. Although this can sometimes worsen your sense of being surrounded by emptiness, it offers you a unique chance to see hostile mobs before they see you.

STRUCTURES

With their surfaces made up mostly of sandstone, structures that generate in deserts blend into the sandy environment. Although they're rare, you could discover pillager outposts, villages and desert pyramids.

It may not look like there's a lot to discover in this uncommon biome, but beyond its sandy surface there is plenty to explore. From suspicious sand blocks, to a structure that is full of mysterious hazards and a unique mob found nowhere else ... let's check out the desert!

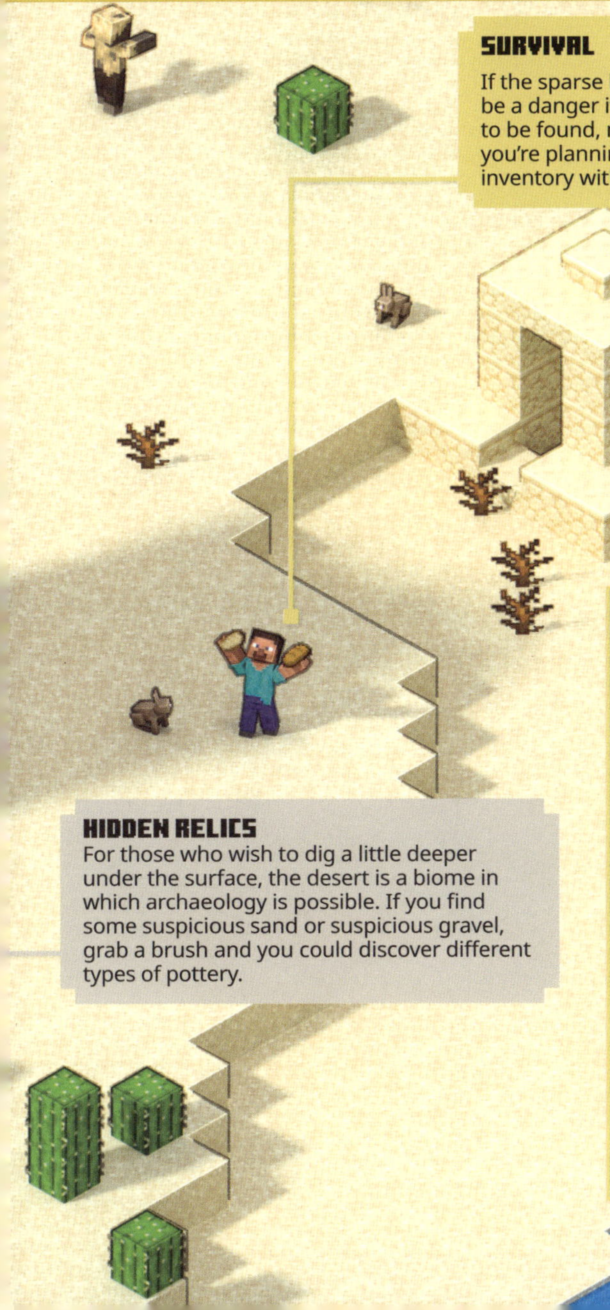

SURVIVAL

If the sparse land helps you spot dangers, it can also be a danger itself. There are little to no resources to be found, meaning survival can be difficult. If you're planning a trip to the desert, try to stock your inventory with wood and food items.

HIDDEN RELICS

For those who wish to dig a little deeper under the surface, the desert is a biome in which archaeology is possible. If you find some suspicious sand or suspicious gravel, grab a brush and you could discover different types of pottery.

MEET THE MOBS

HUSK

There's a good chance you'll witness husks in and around desert pyramids. This variant of zombie only spawns here and will sense you from a lengthy 40 blocks away, so walk with caution. Their damage can inflict the Hunger effect on you.

GENERATED STRUCTURES: DESERT PYRAMID

SANDCASTLES

If you're exploring the desert at night, it would be easy to miss a desert pyramid. Their sandstone towers blend in with their surroundings, so you'll need to look out for their orange terracotta details.

ORANGE TERRACOTTA

PROCEED WITH CAUTION

Keep your wits about you when entering. Hostile mobs have been reported inside, sheltering from the sun.

MEET THE MOBS

SPIDER

Spiders are the only mob that can climb walls, which makes it one to be feared. They attack by jumping, and can bite you in mid-air. Luckily, they only become hostile when it gets dark enough.

TOP TIP

Don't waste time trying to mine the mysterious blocks of suspicious sand. They will only break, unless you use a brush, which will extract an item.

The more time you spend exploring desert biomes, the more you will increase your chances of finding a desert pyramid. These marvellous structures may look like an interesting place to shield from the sun, but the risks of venturing inside can be explosive ...

CREEPED OUT

Explorers with an eye for detail might notice some of the sandstone blocks used for construction have creeper faces etched on their sides. Don't be alarmed – these are just chiselled sandstone blocks, which can also be crafted.

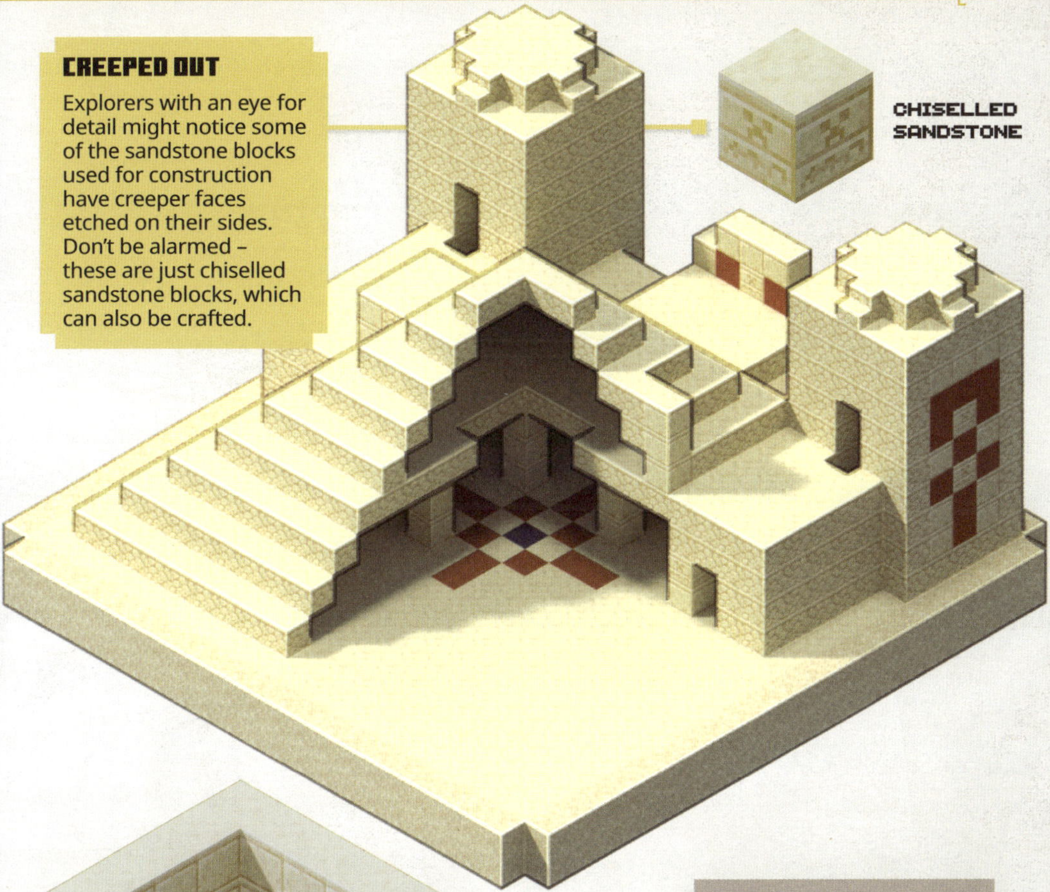

KABOOM

In the centre of the pyramid's main chamber, you will notice a pattern on the floor made up of terracotta. Mine your way below here and you'll be rewarded with a room containing four chests. But do not step on the pressure plate in the centre – it's connected to a 3x3 square of explosive TNT blocks below.

BIOMES: SAVANNAS

There are three types of savanna biomes, all of which are warm in temperature and can usually be found bordering deserts. While they share many similarities, all of them look visually different and offer plenty of reasons to explore.

SAVANNA

WINDSWEPT

PLATEAU

If a savanna generates near higher ground, such as mountains or hills, it could be a plateau variant. These are identical to the regular savanna, but feature a rolling landscape that peaks as it meets other higher biomes.

SAVANNA

The savanna is a mostly flat biome, covered in tall grass and a scattering of acacia and oak trees. It is the only biome in which horses and llamas both spawn. You can use a horse to rapidly explore and a llama to take any items you've collected back to base.

MEET THE MOBS

LLAMA

This mob is one of the best ways of transporting items, but even a tamed llama will refuse to be ridden with a saddle. The best way to guide them is with a lead. Although they're passive, they will spit at anything that causes them harm – and any wolves that stray too close.

BIOMES: BADLANDS

The badlands are an uncommon group of biomes that get their unique colour from red sand and different shades of terracotta. Each looks different to the other, yet they clearly belong together. There's even gold in those hills!

ERODED BADLANDS

Like the other badlands, this variant is covered in red sand, but it looks radically different thanks to the tall spires of terracotta that dominate the landscape. Always explore beyond these, as they may be blocking your view of above-ground mineshafts!

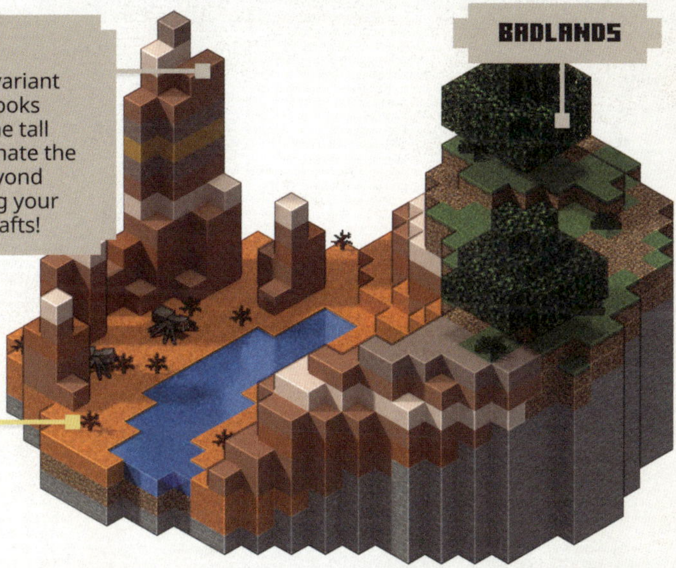

WOODED BADLANDS

This badlands variant has forests of oak trees, which are a great help to anyone who wishes to survive or gather certain resources. It's still a difficult place to explore, with food sources very hard to come by.

ALL THAT GLITTERS

Badlands are a good place to find gold as they are home to more gold than any other biome. Mineshafts also generate frequently – you may even find some jutting out of the sandy red landscape!

HOSTILE SURROUNDS

Passive mobs don't spawn here and there isn't much vegetation, making food hard to find. You'll need to take your own supplies. If you think this means that hostile mobs won't spawn here either, think again!

4

COLD LANDSCAPES

From sea level to the top of the highest snow-covered mountains, cold landscapes offer many of Minecraft's most unique and dangerous exploration opportunities. In this chapter, we'll look at the different landscapes, unique structures and mobs you could encounter in the Overworld's coldest biomes.

BIOMES: WINDSWEPT HILLS

If you're walking among some hills and notice a drop in temperature, you could be in the uncommon and cold family of biomes known as the windswept hills. Bundle up and watch where you step.

WINDSWEPT FOREST

This uncommon biome features forests of oak and spruce trees, that offer a good supply of wood. They can be found on the edge of tall hills that border flatter biomes, causing an increased risk of fall damage.

WINDSWEPT GRAVELLY HILLS

Gravel covers much of the gravelly hills' surface, meaning grass and trees are unable to grow. This biome presents a suffocation risk if you mine from below and get trapped in falling gravel.

WINDSWEPT HILLS

With grassy and stony terrain, you might be forgiven for passing through windswept hills without realising. There are only a few trees and it gets colder higher up, so you might see snowfall and frozen waters.

COW, SHEEP, PIG AND CHICKEN

You will find these four classic mobs across much of the Overworld. Each can be defeated for food and their other drops can provide leather, feathers and wool!

GENERATED STRUCTURES: PILLAGER OUTPOST

When you first approach a pillager outpost, their towers will give you quite a fright. With their imposing dark oak structure and an air of the unknown, only the bravest explorers will choose to enter – but what will they find within?

LOOT

It'll take combat to make it to the top watchtower. Your reward will be a chest that has a 50% chance of containing a crossbow, among other treasures.

DISCOVERY

These outposts can be found across many biomes and are often in close proximity to villages. Thanks to the watchtower at the top, any resident pillagers are likely to spot you approaching long before you make it inside.

BAD OMEN

If you defeat a pillager captain, you'll receive the Bad Omen status effect. Enter a village with this and it will trigger a village raid, sending waves of attacking pillagers in.

MEET THE MOBS

PILLAGERS

You'll find these hostile mobs in outposts and patrolling across the Overworld. Their aim with a crossbow is precise and they will attack adult villagers ... and you.

BIOMES: TAIGA

These grasslands are great for new cold biome explorers. They are chilly, but forests of ferns and spruce trees provide wood to gather. Snowy taigas are similar, but are covered in a layer of snow and you could find an igloo!

OLD GROWTH TAIGA

Thanks to their great age, the spruce or pine trees in old growth taigas have grown distinctively tall. As a result of the high humidity levels in this biome, there's a good chance that you'll discover a lush cave (see page 71) somewhere below ground there, so ensure you have mining and survival supplies to explore underground.

SNOWY TAIGA

TAIGA

MEET THE MOBS

FOXES

This elusive mob can be spotted in taigas, dozing peacefully in the sun. It can also be seen leaping through the air to attack its prey ... which isn't quite so peaceful.

GENERATED STRUCTURES:
IGLOO

Found in snowy biomes and built with snowy blocks, igloos can be easy to miss. But while their exteriors might seem small and simple, their interiors offer solace to travellers and excitement to explorers.

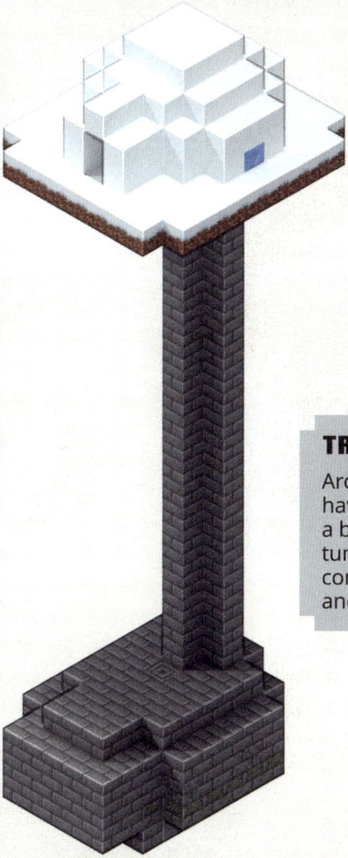

STRUCTURE

On entering an igloo, you will find immediate cover from the freezing weather. A room containing a bed, furnace and crafting table is useful, but the real excitement could be hidden from your view ...

TRAPDOOR

Around half of igloos generated will have a hidden trapdoor underneath a block of carpet. This leads down a tunnel and to a basement chamber, containing a brewing stand, a cauldron and a chest ... and mysterious cells.

PRISONERS?

The basement cells contain two unlikely neighbours. In one, a villager awaits freedom, in the other, a zombie villager. Will you cure them with a golden apple?

BIOMES: SNOWY PLAINS

A visual delight to explore, snowy plains are mostly covered in pristine white snow and towering icy formations. Survival can be difficult, thanks to a lack of mobs and powder snow that can cause freeze damage.

STRUCTURES

Although rare, structures can be found by explorers. Village buildings made of wood stand out and offer warmth and shelter from the testing elements.

NATURAL COLOURS

While much of the snowy plains are covered in white snow, any exposed grass is aqua green in colour. Ice is in abundance here and any rivers or lakes will be frozen over, unless a natural lava lake is close by.

SURVIVAL

The layers of snow might make this hard to believe, but the snowy plains are grasslands. The climate makes trees quite a rare occurrence, making the whole biome appear barren – not helped by the small number of mobs that spawn here.

MEET THE MOBS

POLAR BEAR

Although rare, this majestic mob can be found in icy biomes. Keep your distance, or they will rear on their back legs and maul you with their front claws!

BIOMES:
ICE SPIKES

There are some places in the Overworld that must be seen to be believed, and one of them is the ice spikes biome. It's an awe-inspiring sight, covered in groups of out-of-this-world spikes.

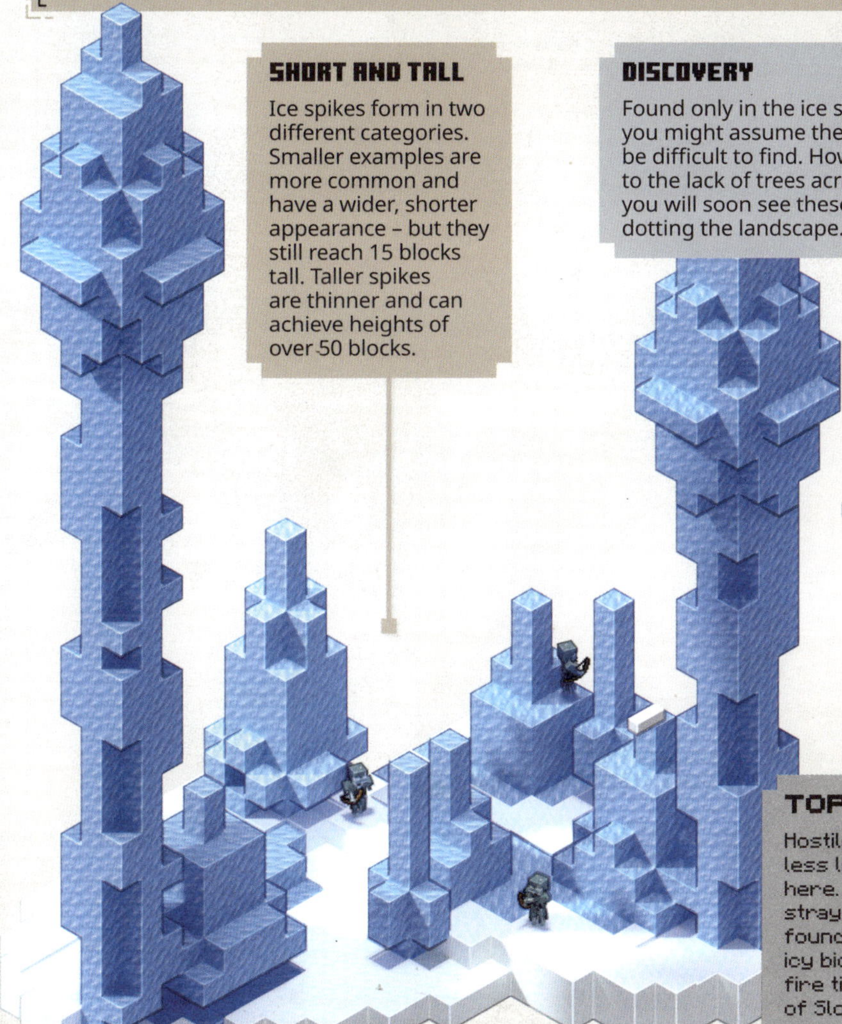

SHORT AND TALL

Ice spikes form in two different categories. Smaller examples are more common and have a wider, shorter appearance – but they still reach 15 blocks tall. Taller spikes are thinner and can achieve heights of over 50 blocks.

DISCOVERY

Found only in the ice spikes biome, you might assume these spires will be difficult to find. However, thanks to the lack of trees across the biome, you will soon see these large turrets dotting the landscape.

TOP TIP

Hostile mobs are less likely to spawn here. However, strays can be found wandering icy biomes. They fire tipped arrows of Slowness, which will slow you down!

BIOMES: SLOPES

Seeing that you're approaching some mountainous terrain means you may have some serious walking and climbing coming up. Let it also be a warning to stock up on supplies – you might be busy for the next few days.

GROVE

If the mountainsides have rich forests of spruce trees, you might have climbed into a grove biome. Snow can settle here, giving it an unpredictable appearance.

MEADOW

Found on the lower edges of mountains, meadows are the only mountainous biome in which villages generate – a perfect base for planning an expedition.

MEET THE MOBS

RABBIT

It's rare to witness this shy mob. If you manage to defeat a rabbit, you could get some raw meat to use in a stew, and a rabbit's foot, used in a potion of Leaping.

SNOWY SLOPES

Snowy slopes are a desolate place. The bare, ridged slopes contain strips of powder snow and the odd screaming goat waiting to ram you.

BIOMES: PEAKS

At the very top of mountains, where the cool, crisp air is as sharp as some of the potential drops, you will find three peak biomes. These are found nowhere else and offer some of the most dramatic landscapes in the Overworld.

FROZEN PEAKS

Adventuring into any of the peaks is only for the bravest explorers who have prepared well. The frozen peaks may have smaller and smoother hills to navigate, but they have treacherous glaciers of packed ice – so tread carefully.

STONY PEAKS

If a mountain is close to savannas and jungles, it generates as a stony peak. These feature rocky hills with exposed ores to tempt brave mountain climbers higher.

JAGGED PEAKS

This biome's tall and jagged peaks, can climb high above the level of clouds. Across its surface is a layer of snow, under which you can dig to find ores. You'll need to navigate carefully to avoid fall damage.

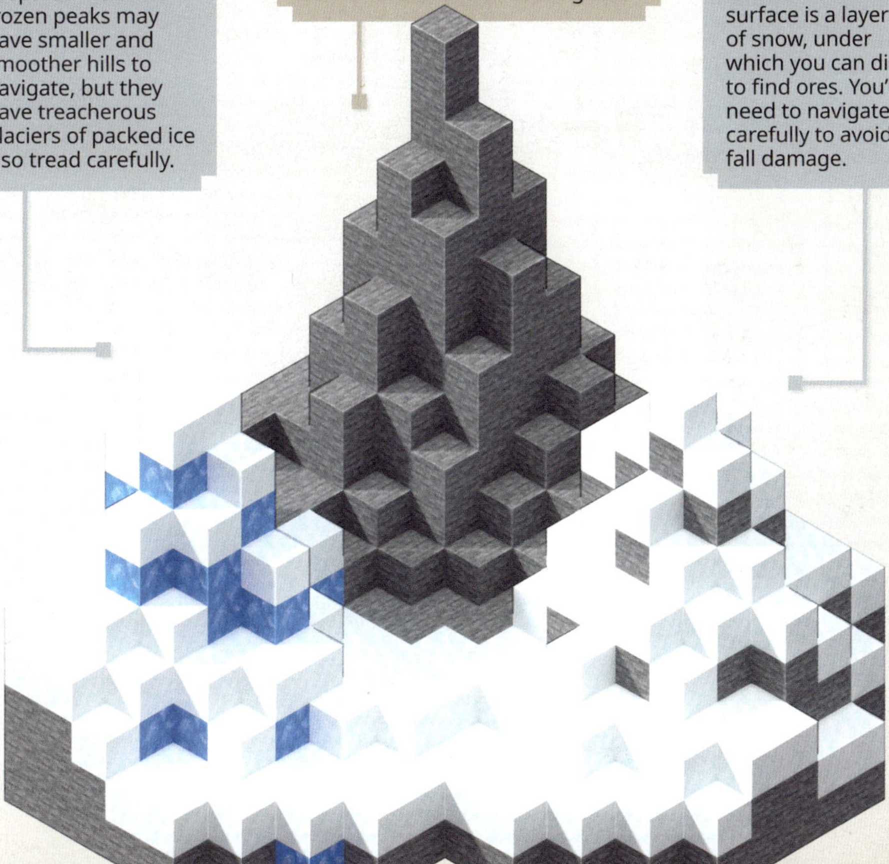

5

AQUATIC LANDSCAPES

Water covers much of the Overworld's surface, so you won't need to look far to find an aquatic biome. These intriguing places appeal to the explorer within us all, but by their very nature they are some of the most difficult biomes to survive in. Let's jump below their surface and discover a world of mystery.

RIVERS

DANGERS OF EXPLORATION

There's much to explore under the surface. You will spot resources from the riverbank, but the intriguing entrances to huge underwater caves could lead to many other riches. You can only hold your breath for so long, so be aware of your oxygen level!

DID YOU KNOW?

Boats can carry you and a chest, and are the fastest way to travel on water. But be warned, some rivers flow in one big circle – so you'll end where you started.

You will find rivers winding across the Overworld's surface. Sometimes their position creates a natural border between biomes, and often they will eventually lead you to oceans. While they might look calm on the surface, they can harbour hostile mobs and much to discover below.

DEPTH

Many rivers are similar in depth and you can normally see to the bottom of their riverbeds. In mountainous areas, their depths can increase and some are as deep as oceans – making them more difficult to survey.

RESOURCES

Rivers are a source of several useful items and resources. You don't need to craft a fishing rod to catch fish, which will replenish your hunger bar, raw or cooked. Also, in their shallower waters, breaking gravel can give you flint and you may find clay blocks.

MEET THE MOBS

DROWNED

If you've ever explored underwater, then you will likely have witnessed these zombie variants. Like zombies, they will attack through melee bashes, but some spawn with one of the most damaging weapons in the Overworld: the trident.

BIOMES: MUSHROOM FIELDS

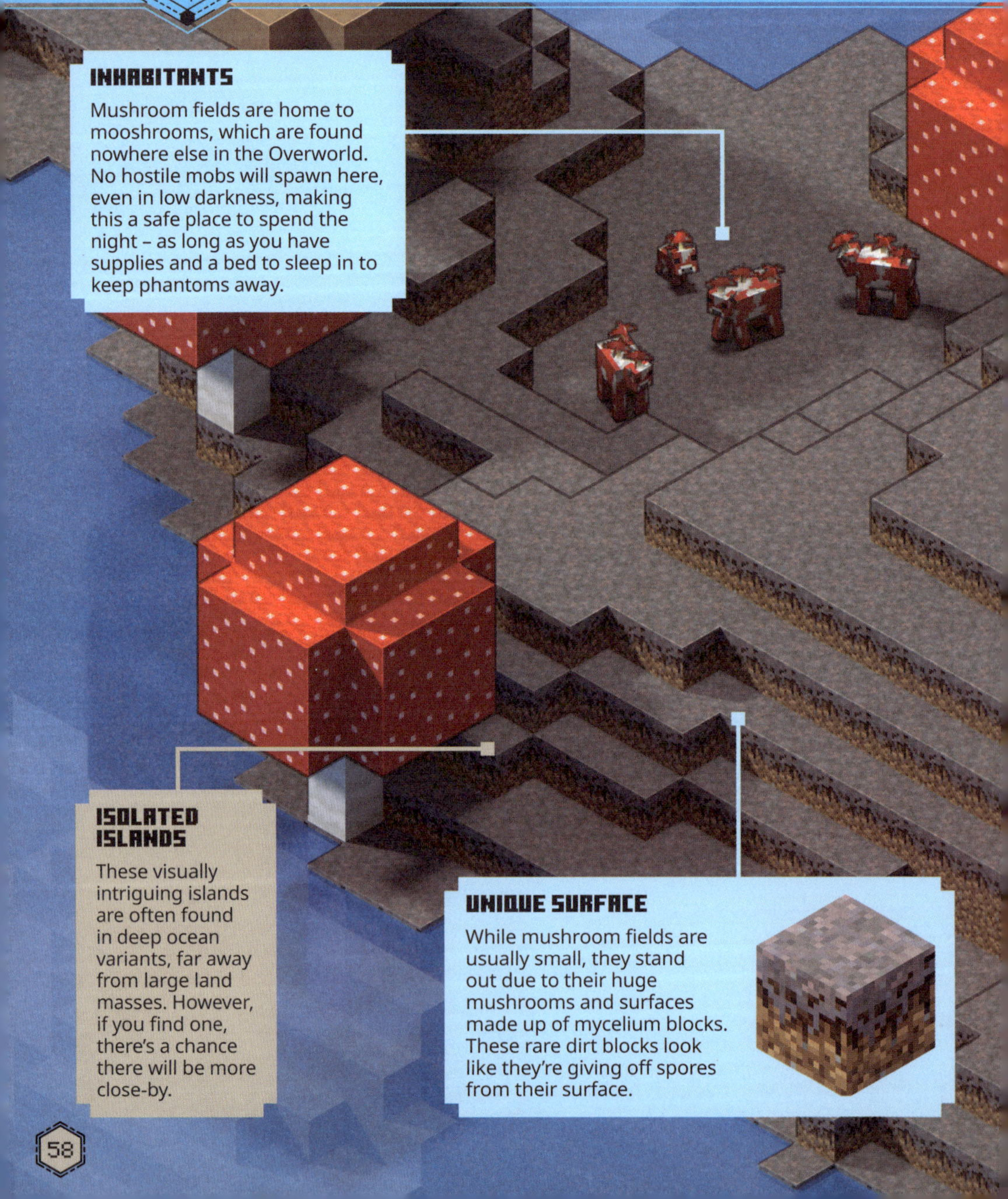

INHABITANTS

Mushroom fields are home to mooshrooms, which are found nowhere else in the Overworld. No hostile mobs will spawn here, even in low darkness, making this a safe place to spend the night – as long as you have supplies and a bed to sleep in to keep phantoms away.

ISOLATED ISLANDS

These visually intriguing islands are often found in deep ocean variants, far away from large land masses. However, if you find one, there's a chance there will be more close-by.

UNIQUE SURFACE

While mushroom fields are usually small, they stand out due to their huge mushrooms and surfaces made up of mycelium blocks. These rare dirt blocks look like they're giving off spores from their surface.

There comes a time in every seafaring explorer's life when they approach an island and realise they've got no idea what they've discovered. This is often the case with mushroom fields, whose giant mushrooms add unexpected colour to this biome.

MEET THE MOBS

MOOSHROOM

Mooshrooms look like cows, but are almost always red and covered in mushrooms. You can breed them, milk them and even shear them for mushrooms – though this would transform them into just a regular cow.

OCEANS

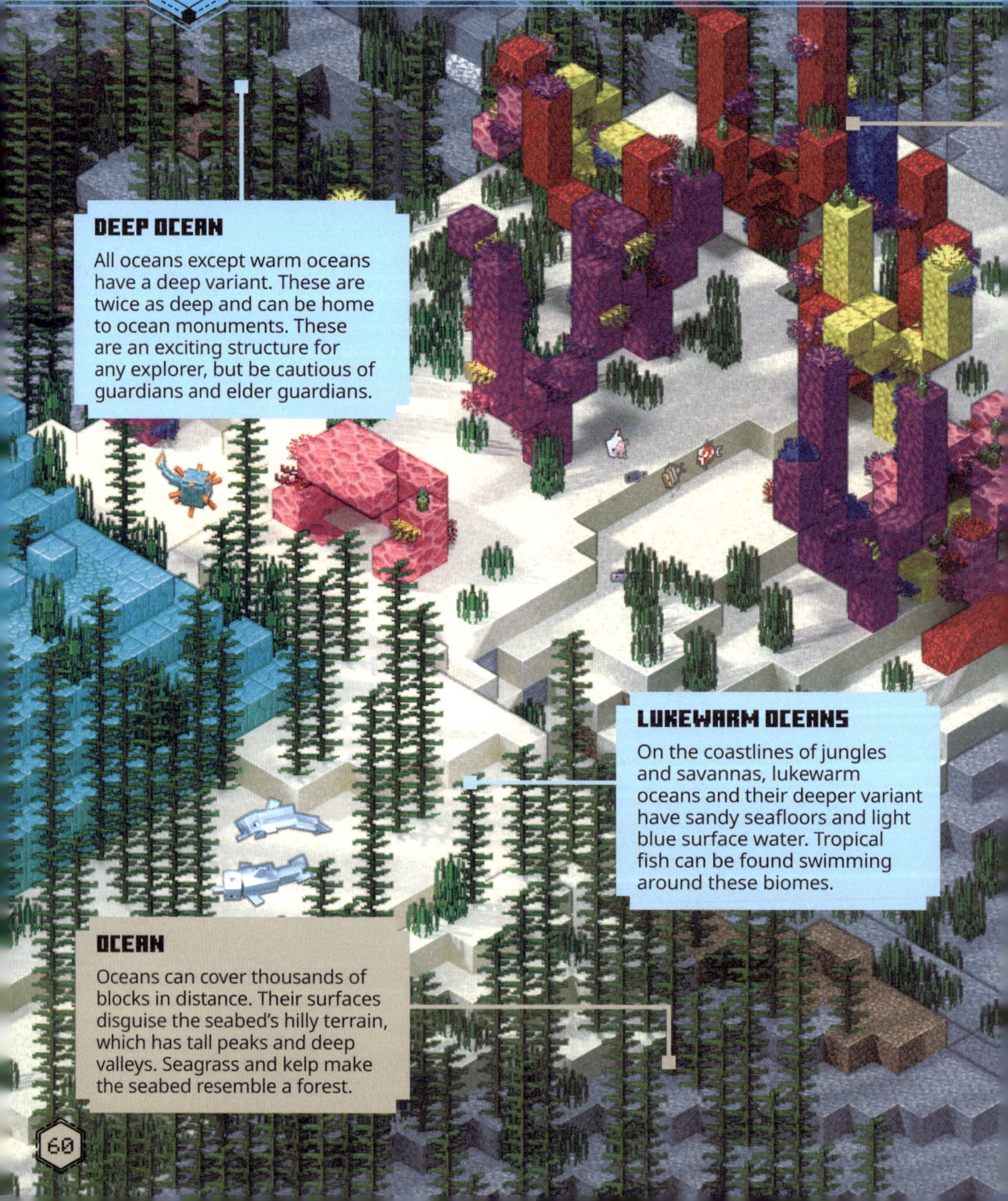

DEEP OCEAN

All oceans except warm oceans have a deep variant. These are twice as deep and can be home to ocean monuments. These are an exciting structure for any explorer, but be cautious of guardians and elder guardians.

LUKEWARM OCEANS

On the coastlines of jungles and savannas, lukewarm oceans and their deeper variant have sandy seafloors and light blue surface water. Tropical fish can be found swimming around these biomes.

OCEAN

Oceans can cover thousands of blocks in distance. Their surfaces disguise the seabed's hilly terrain, which has tall peaks and deep valleys. Seagrass and kelp make the seabed resemble a forest.

Covering the largest area of any biome, oceans might look sparse on the surface, but they offer a huge underwater world to explore. From vast trenches to undiscovered shipwrecks, there is so much to see and many dangers to survive.

WARM OCEAN

Warm oceans can be found bordering deserts and badlands. You can recognise these from the aquamarine water tones and colourful array of unique coral that generate here.

FROZEN OCEAN

Under the surface, frozen and deep frozen oceans have a gravel seabed that is empty and barren. Although the surface is mostly frozen, you might be lucky enough to witness one of nature's wonders – a giant floating iceberg with a polar bear on it.

MEET THE MOBS

DOLPHIN

This neutral mob will grant a speed boost if you sprint-swim near it. Its ability to jump is amazing, but its real skill is only displayed if you feed it one raw cod or raw salmon. It will swim to the nearest shipwreck, buried treasure or ocean monument! Quick, follow it!

COLD OCEAN

With a darker shade of water on its surface, the cold ocean biome looks noticeably different to the warmer ocean variants. You will find less seagrass on the sea floor than those too, but the same mobs can be found swimming around – or waiting for you.

GENERATED STRUCTURES: SHIPWRECK

DANGERS

As with any underwater voyages, there are some simple dangers to be aware of. Try not to get caught out by a drowned with a trident and always keep an eye on your oxygen bar – don't get trapped within the wreck.

ESSENTIAL TOOL

Consider crafting a turtle shell when exploring underwater structures. It will grant you 2 armour points and an extra 10 seconds of Water Breathing every time you dive below the surface, offering you invaluable aquatic assistance.

Turtle shell recipe

One of the most exciting discoveries any explorer can make is the shipwreck. Found in all ocean biomes, these rare structures can be seen in or near water, sometimes with their masts protruding from the surface and sometimes keeled on their sides, or even upside down. Ahoy there!

STRUCTURE

Shipwrecks can generate in different ways and varying levels of damage. Some are upright and intact; some are keeled sideways with damage, and some are upside down so they can be difficult to recognise.

DISCOVERY

Shipwrecks are rare structures so can be hard to find. Using a dolphin to locate one saves time, but nothing comes close to the thrill of finding one yourself. They can sometimes be found above water on beaches or snowy beaches and even sometimes in icebergs or ravines, so if you're lucky, you may just stumble across one on your adventures.

TREASURES

No shipwreck would be complete without some treasures to loot. You can find as many as three chests inside, with one in the bow, and one in each of the upper and lower sections of the stern. If there are at least two chests, one of these will be a map chest containing a map to buried treasure!

GENERATED STRUCTURES: OCEAN RUINS

Ocean ruins are a collection of oceanic structures that come in many different shapes and sizes. Whether it's a single ruin or a large village, there's always a reason to explore behind their walls.

COMPOSITION

Depending on the climate, ocean ruins will be made of different materials. In cold biomes, they will be constructed of stone bricks. In warmer climates, they can be made of sandstone, helping them blend in with their surroundings.

BURIED

An ocean ruin may not look like much, but don't move on just yet – many have chests buried underneath. Also keep an eye out for suspicious sand, which could contain the eggs of an ancient mob: the sniffer!

DROWNED

If you are near an ocean ruin, there's a good chance drowned will be nearby, with many spawning close to these mysterious structures. If you focus too much on uncovering a chest or sniffer eggs, they may take you by surprise.

GENERATED STRUCTURES: OCEAN MONUMENT

If you are exploring beneath the surface of a deep ocean variant, you may catch sight of a rare ocean monument. These enormous structures are full of chambers, containing several threats and some rare rewards.

LOCATION

Due to their size, ocean monuments are not difficult to spot from afar by any explorers who have spent some time in the ocean. However, to speed up your search, you could use an explorer map to locate one, available from cartographer villagers. See pages 20-21 for more information on maps.

DANGERS

It's easy to get trapped and disoriented, so it would be foolish to ever attempt to explore one without Water Breathing aid. This structure doesn't come undefended: it's patrolled by the formidable elder guardians and guardians.

PRISMARINE

Ocean monuments have a very unique appearance with a rare prismarine structure. Survive their complex combination of chambers and you could unearth a treasure chamber containing 8 blocks of gold, and a curious sponge room.

MEET THE MOBS

GUARDIAN AND ELDER GUARDIAN

These hostile mobs will attack by firing laser beams at you and, if you touch them at all, they will retaliate with their spikes. The grey elder guardian is the biggest and strongest aquatic mob and you'll find three inside an ocean monument.

6

UNDERGROUND LANDSCAPES

Below the Overworld's surface, there's a whole world waiting to be explored, but be warned: you must proceed with caution. All of your survival skills will be put to the test, as you traverse sprawling networks of caves full of jaw-dropping sights and teeming with hostile mobs.

GOING UNDERGROUND

GETTING STARTED

Underground is a dangerous place to explore. To be prepared, you must store all your valuables above ground and only take lots of essentials down with you.

SPARE BLOCKS

Spare blocks can be used to descend, cross deep valleys and even create defensive walls to keep hostile mobs away. Try to take down at least one whole stack of dirt or cobblestone.

MAKE YOUR MARK

Try to keep a note of your coordinates. If you're defeated without sleeping in a bed, you might struggle to find the location again. To turn coordinates on, go to world options in the main menu.

Mining is essential for the gathering of valuable resources and rare items that can transform your experiences back on the surface. You might not plan on it, but adventures underground can last for days on end, as you search caves, mineshafts and incredible underground structures.

LISTEN UP

Turn up the volume. When underground, you will often hear nearby mobs or even the sound of dripping water or lava, which can help you avoid threats and locate hidden discoveries.

DEEP SLEEP

The deeper you explore, the more chances there are that you will lose your way and meet an untimely end. Place a bed and sleep in it, so you will respawn closer – just remember to sleep somewhere else once you make it back above ground.

An iron pickaxe is capable of breaking the most valuable ores, such as gold and diamond.

Torches are essential for lighting up dark caves and finding your way back out.

Use a stone sword for close-combat defence. It isn't the strongest – but it's easy to craft when you are lacking resources.

Weapons will need replacing and furnaces will need fuel. Wood planks are multi-purpose.

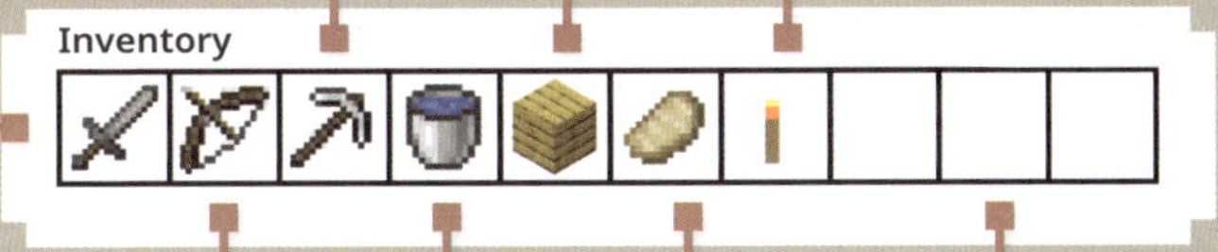

Creating a waterfall with a water bucket will help you travel safely down deep drops – and back up.

Keep lots of slots empty to carry any valuables you gather back to the surface.

Caves are teeming with skeletons. Defend yourself and fight back with a bow.

There's no food in caves, so a stash of food will help keep your hunger away.

CAVES

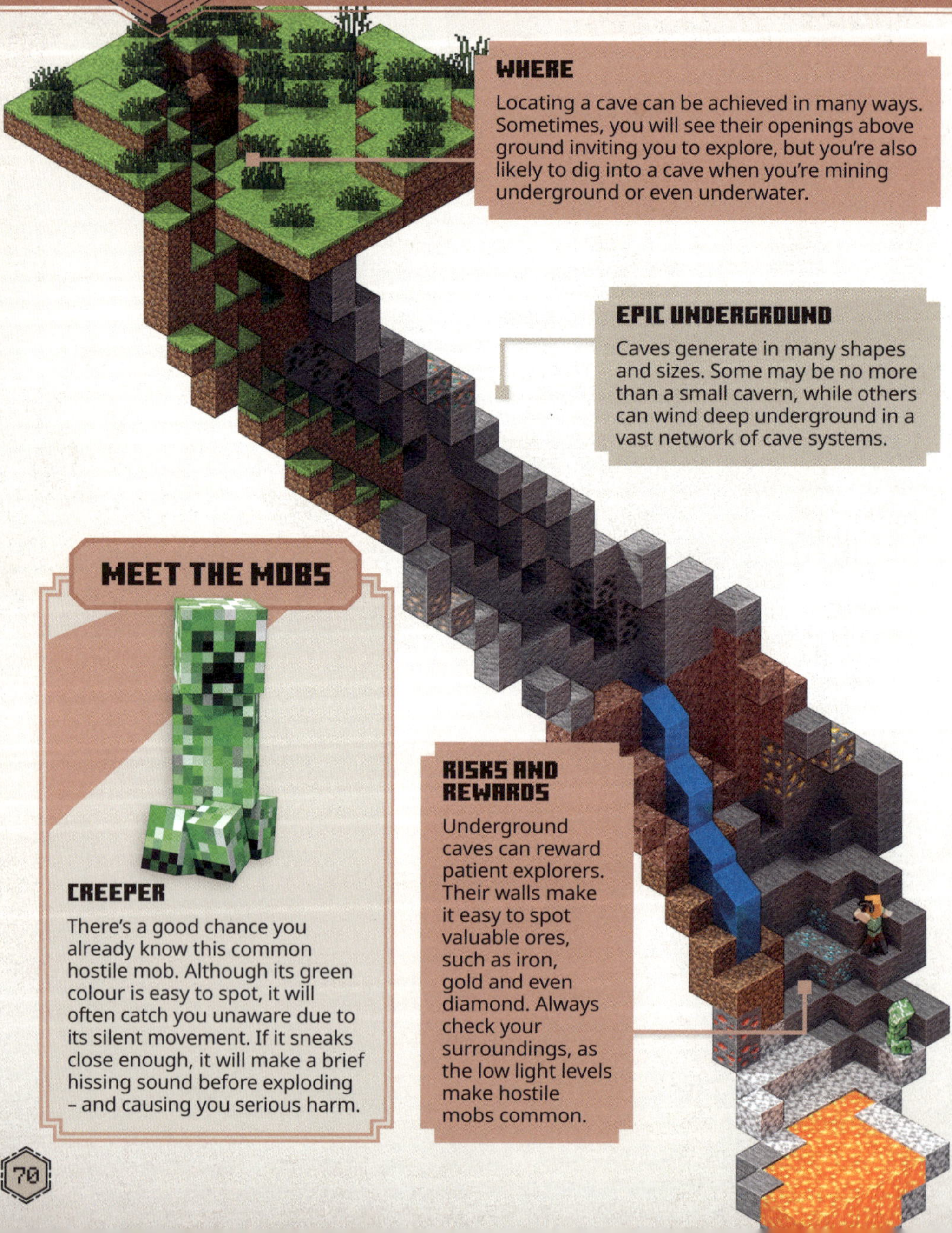

WHERE

Locating a cave can be achieved in many ways. Sometimes, you will see their openings above ground inviting you to explore, but you're also likely to dig into a cave when you're mining underground or even underwater.

EPIC UNDERGROUND

Caves generate in many shapes and sizes. Some may be no more than a small cavern, while others can wind deep underground in a vast network of cave systems.

MEET THE MOBS

CREEPER

There's a good chance you already know this common hostile mob. Although its green colour is easy to spot, it will often catch you unaware due to its silent movement. If it sneaks close enough, it will make a brief hissing sound before exploding – and causing you serious harm.

RISKS AND REWARDS

Underground caves can reward patient explorers. Their walls make it easy to spot valuable ores, such as iron, gold and even diamond. Always check your surroundings, as the low light levels make hostile mobs common.

Caves can keep any explorer busy for hours, if not days, on end. Even if you can't see a cave opening nearby, you are never far away from an underground adventure. A little bit of digging could see you return to the surface with an inventory full of exciting new riches.

CAVES

Although there are different types of cave, the common variant is widespread and easy to recognise. Some offer large spaces that invite you to explore with ease, while others have narrow and jagged corridors that require careful navigation to avoid becoming trapped or attacked.

LUSH CAVES

If you're in a humid biome then look out for lush caves, which can often be found below azalea trees. These are covered in moss, moss carpets, azalea bushes and hanging vines of glow berries. You may even spot scurrying axolotls, too.

DEEP DARK

Far underground, with almost no source of light, the deep dark is covered in sculk blocks, surrounded with sculk veins. Sculk sensors disturbed more than five times can trigger sculk shriekers, and you'll run the risk of meeting the warden. This is the only biome in which ancient cities can be found.

DRIPSTONE CAVES

Often found inland, their large dripstone stalactites and stalagmites and dripstone surface create hazardous navigation, and can cause you damage if you fall on to them. Large amounts of copper ore can be found here, as well as a high occurrence of amethyst geodes – so gather what you can.

GENERATED STRUCTURES: MINESHAFT

LARGE COMPLEXES

Mineshafts can vary in size and even generate near each other, to form large underground complexes. This can make them difficult to navigate, so try to take a stack of torches with you to use as markers.

WALKWAYS

When mineshafts generate in and around deep caves, they may have wooden walkways that reach over deep canyons. These can help you safely navigate dangerous terrain and can save you from losing your way – but they can also benefit hostile mobs who wish to pursue you.

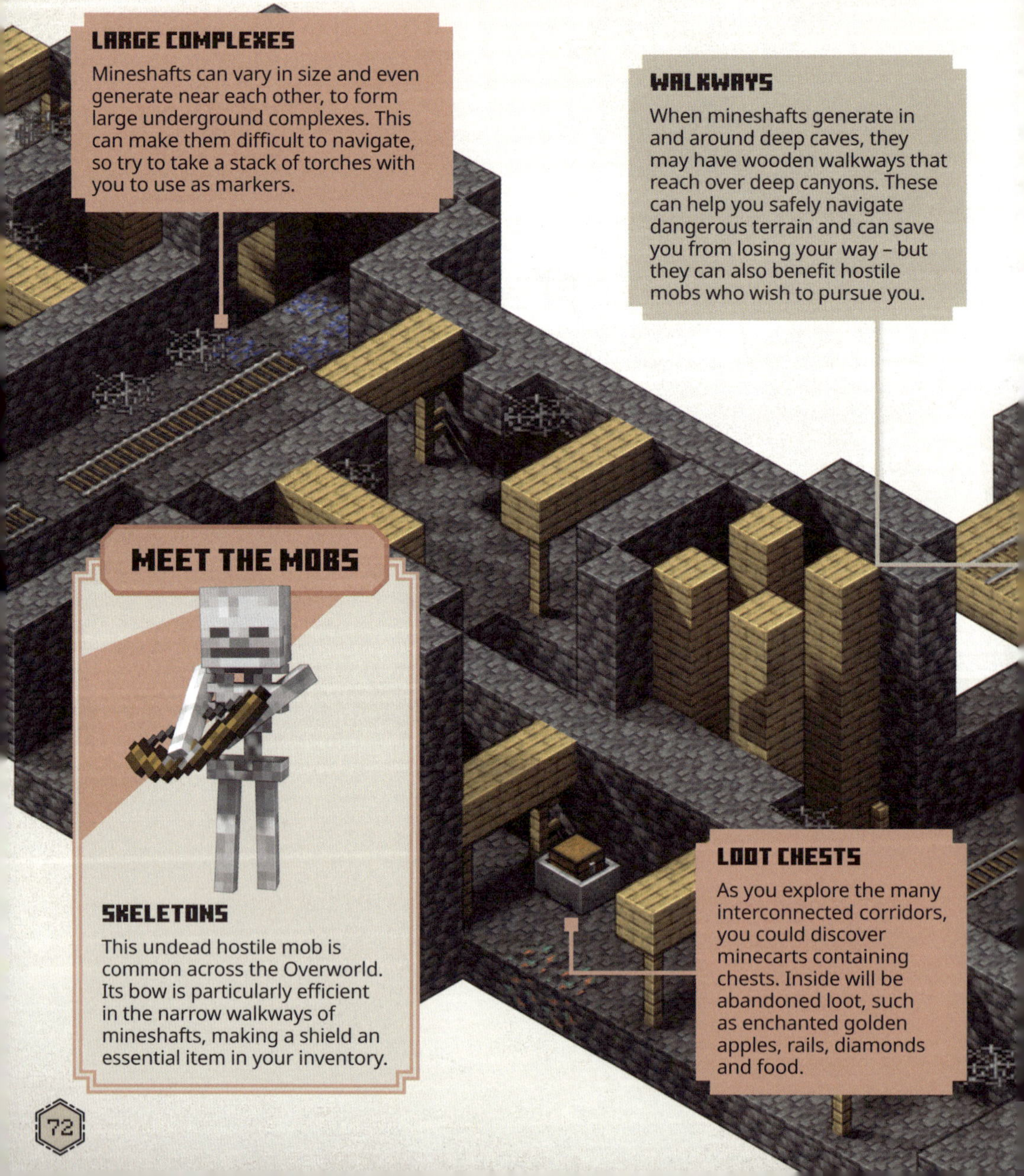

MEET THE MOBS

SKELETONS

This undead hostile mob is common across the Overworld. Its bow is particularly efficient in the narrow walkways of mineshafts, making a shield an essential item in your inventory.

LOOT CHESTS

As you explore the many interconnected corridors, you could discover minecarts containing chests. Inside will be abandoned loot, such as enchanted golden apples, rails, diamonds and food.

Found primarily in underground caves, mineshafts are maze-like structures made up of tunnel networks. They contain many incomplete rail lines and an abundance of oak plank platforms, giving them a distinct appearance that stands out underground.

MOBS

The long, dark corridors of a mineshaft are the perfect place for hostile mobs to spawn and catch you by surprise. Preparation is key, so a sword, a bow and a shield are essential items.

ABANDONED PASSAGEWAYS

If you have shears, use them to break away the thick layers of cobwebs found here. But be warned, cave spider monster spawners are often concealed inside. Break these with a pickaxe to stop the flow of spiders.

IN THE BADLANDS

In the badlands biome, evidence of mineshafts can sometimes be witnessed above ground. If you spot their dark oak colours then it might be wise to explore – the badlands are an excellent place to find gold ore.

GENERATED STRUCTURES: STRONGHOLD

Strongholds are one of the most sought-after structures in the Overworld, and for good reason. Their walls contain a maze of passageways and secrets, and are home to a portal to reach the End dimension.

HOW TO FIND THEM

Due to their underground locations, strongholds are difficult to find. You can discover one by chance, but you could also use an eye of Ender. Throw one and it will travel about 12 blocks in the direction of the nearest stronghold.

ROOMS

There are several spaces inside. Cells line some walls, corridors can contain chests and one room contains a decorative fountain. Low light levels mean hostile mobs are a common sight.

LIBRARY

Strongholds often contain libraries. They come in two sizes, from a smaller, single level room to a larger, two storey library. Inside both, you will find bookshelves, oak planks and a chest or two.

END PORTAL

The only place you can find an End portal is in a stronghold's portal room. Every explorer wants to find one, but be warned: every portal room has a hostile silverfish spawner within.

GENERATED STRUCTURES: ANCIENT CITY

In the darkness of the deep dark biome can be found a sprawling structure known as an ancient city. It might be hard to make out all the detail in the darkness, but explore with caution and you'll uncover ancient secrets.

STATUES

Stood in eternal darkness, the numerous statues can catch you by surprise. Especially at the centre, where a large statue resembling a warden's head stands overlooking the corridors.

UNIQUE TREASURES

Several elements in an ancient city can be found nowhere else. The structure is made of reinforced deepslate, a block that cannot be broken by your tools. But soul lanterns and echo shards can be picked up and taken with you.

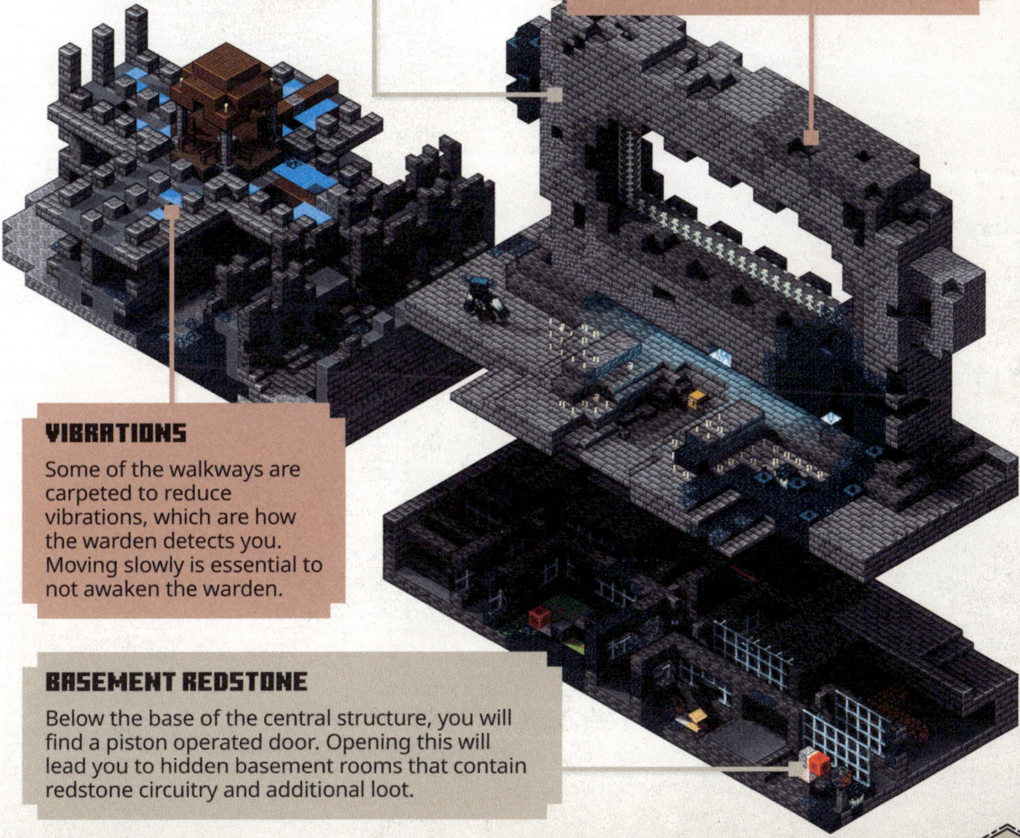

VIBRATIONS

Some of the walkways are carpeted to reduce vibrations, which are how the warden detects you. Moving slowly is essential to not awaken the warden.

BASEMENT REDSTONE

Below the base of the central structure, you will find a piston operated door. Opening this will lead you to hidden basement rooms that contain redstone circuitry and additional loot.

7

THE NETHER

Although there's more than enough to explore across the Overworld, the bravest of explorers can attempt to reach the Nether. This lava-filled dimension is not for the faint of heart, and contains a whole new world of natural threats and hostile mobs.

TRAVELLING TO THE NETHER

In order to travel to the Nether dimension, a player must first create a Nether portal. Crafted using obsidian blocks, these glowing structures are gateways to another world that is unlike anywhere else.

BE PREPARED

Don't let excitement cloud your judgement. Be prepared with food, weapons, gold armour and some gold ingots to trade with piglins.

OBSIDIAN

You can find obsidian across all dimensions. It is created when water flows over a lava source, and is so tough that it can only be broken and gathered with a diamond pickaxe. You will need a minimum of 10 blocks to craft your own Nether portal.

LIGHT IT UP

Once you've built an obsidian frame, use a flint and steel to activate the portal. Other fire sources work too, such as a fire charge. To use your portal, stand inside the frame for four seconds.

NETHER PORTAL STAGES

TOP TIP

A portal will work without the corners filled in with obsidian blocks.

BIOMES:
NETHER WASTES

Nothing can prepare you for your first visit to the Nether. The most common biome is the Nether wastes, a barren landscape covered in netherrack, strange new mobs and unique dangers.

DEEP GLOW

Although it's a dark and gloomy place, the lakes and waterfalls of lava and hanging clusters of glowstone provide a light source. Glowstone can be broken and gathered to use as a unique decorative block.

SPAWN AGAIN

If you've made it to the Nether, then you know that a bed is the best security against losing your progress. However, if you try to sleep in a bed in the Nether, it will explode ... with you in it!

DANGERS

There are many mobs in the Nether, and some of them won't be happy to see you. Simply running from them is difficult, thanks to the many lava pits that break up the Nether's landscape.

MEET THE MOBS

PIGLINS

Although they are a neutral mob, piglins will turn hostile unless you have an item of gold armour equipped. They are obsessed with gold, and you can even trade it with them for interesting items, such as Ender pearls.

BIOMES: NETHER FORESTS

CRIMSON FOREST

HARD TO SEE

You will know when you've discovered a crimson forest, thanks to its dense fungi and dark red fog. It's certainly one of the most fearful places any explorer can experience, but it has to be seen to be believed.

HANGING OUT

A crimson forest has an interesting variety of vegetation, including huge crimson fungi, which resemble trees. On the forest ceilings, weeping vines hang from the Nether wart blocks. Weeping vines can be collected and used for interesting decoration back in the Overworld.

ABLAZE

Don't be alarmed by the blazing particles you will discover floating in the air. They can't cause you harm – but any lava lakes should be avoided, because they really can!

MEET THE MOBS

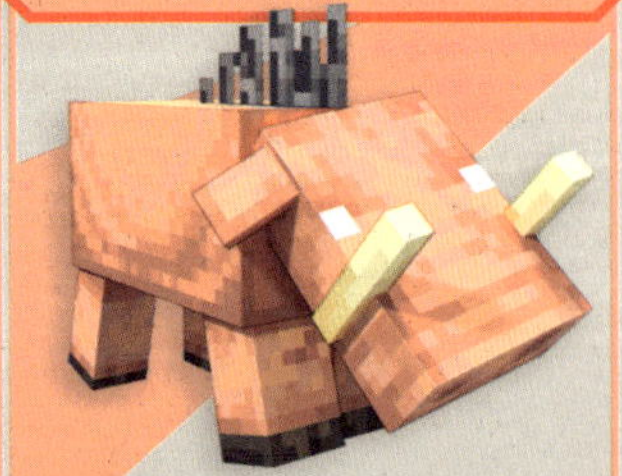

HOGLIN

One mob native to the crimson forest is the hoglin. Found in herds of three or four, they are hostile and intend to cause you harm. If you defeat one, they will drop 2-4 porkchops – a very rare source of food in the Nether.

Many explorers feel a sense of doom in the Nether and worry they will never escape its wastes. Those brave enough to continue may discover unique new terrains, such as two Nether forest variants: the crimson forest and the warped forest. Let's see what you will find there.

WARPED FOREST

A SAFE PLACE?

They aren't free of danger, but warped forests spawn no hostile mobs. Endermen won't cause you harm unless you stare at them and the striders seen walking on lava lakes are passive.

FOGGY VISION

This forest gets its name from the warped nylium that covers much of its terrain. This teal-coloured block is a variant of the netherrack that covers much of the Nether and gives the warped forest an eery darkness.

A TWIST

You won't find any natural food sources in warped forests, though there is other vegetation. Look out for twisting vines, which can be broken and collected. They can be placed for climbing, and will even slow down any accidental drops, preventing fall damage.

MEET THE MOBS

STRIDER

Striders spawn above lava and can be ridden, enabling you to cross lava lakes and access remote locations. You'll need to saddle it first, and can direct it using a warped fungus on a stick. While they thrive on lava, they struggle on dry land.

BIOMES: SOUL SAND VALLEY

The Nether is made of large cavernous areas, but none are as distinctive as soul sand valleys. Made up of Nether fossils and rare blocks, such as soul sand and soul soil, there is nowhere else that looks like these valleys.

FOSSILS

Visible throughout soul sand valleys are Nether fossils. Sometimes incredibly large, these mysterious fossils only add to the ghostly feeling any explorer will experience here.

IN THE AIR

By all accounts, a soul sand valley is one of the scariest places an explorer can try to find. Its foggy, greenish-blue atmosphere is full of the sound of blowing winds and the many whispers they carry.

SOUL SAND

Soul sand slows you down but it'll slow mobs, too. It's also a tool for building water lifts, as it gives off a bubble column that can push you up through the water.

MEET THE MOBS

GHAST

These ghost-like flying mobs are extremely hostile, so don't stare for too long. Don't be fooled by their crying sounds – if you walk into their range, they will spit powerful fireballs at you!

BIOMES:
BASALT DELTAS

One of the most dangerous places to travel to in all of the Overworld and the Nether combined, basalt deltas should be avoided at all costs. But things aren't always that simple, are they?

TERRAIN

Basalt deltas are visually striking, which is what makes them so dangerous. Their jagged cliffs and hidden lava pools have resulted in the demise of many an explorer before you, so walk with care and try not to get bumped into.

MEET THE MOBS

MAGMA CUBE

Although it looks different to a slime, a magma cube behaves in much the same way. However, it can jump higher and cause you more damage as it bounces around and tries to bump into you.

MAGMA CREAM

One of the potential loot opportunities here comes in the form of magma cream. Dropped by magma cubes, it can be collected and used to brew potions of Fire Resistance and to craft magma blocks, which can be used as a light source – just don't step on one!

GENERATED STRUCTURES: BASTION REMNANT

These epic castle-like structures are truly a sight to behold. You can find them all across the Nether, except in basalt deltas, and while there are four variants, there is no mistaking when you witness one of them.

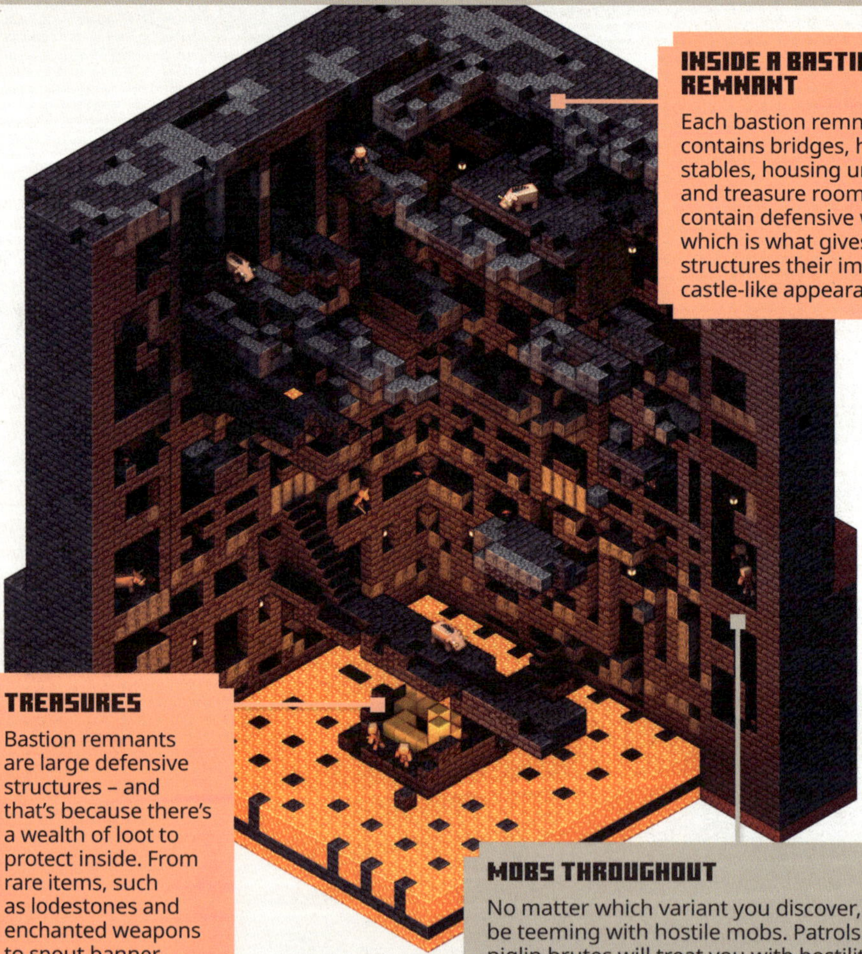

INSIDE A BASTION REMNANT

Each bastion remnant contains bridges, hoglin stables, housing units and treasure rooms. All contain defensive walls, which is what gives these structures their immense castle-like appearance.

TREASURES

Bastion remnants are large defensive structures – and that's because there's a wealth of loot to protect inside. From rare items, such as lodestones and enchanted weapons to snout banner patterns to take home and decorate your farm with!

MOBS THROUGHOUT

No matter which variant you discover, it will be teeming with hostile mobs. Patrols of piglin brutes will treat you with hostility, even if you are wearing gold armour. One hard hit could put your entire journey at risk, so always stay aware of your surroundings.

GENERATED STRUCTURES: NETHER FORTRESS

As its name suggests, Nether fortresses are terrifying structures, found all across the Nether. Their bridges, corridors and towers can be difficult to navigate and are heavily guarded by some exclusive mobs.

NETHER FORTRESS

Nether fortresses are made of Nether bricks, and are one of the hardest generated structures you can attempt to conquer.

MEET THE MOBS

BLAZE

The blaze is a floating hostile mob with a fireball trio attack that causes serious damage. Manage to defeat one and you could be rewarded with a blaze rod – the sole ingredient to craft blaze powder, which is an essential fuel for brewing potions.

SPAWN SPEED

Nether fortresses are home to blazes and Wither skeletons – two mobs that can't be found elsewhere. They can also have a higher number of mobs spawning than usual, so you'll have to call on all of your exploring experience to escape a Nether fortress.

LOOT

Brave explorers who conquer a Nether fortress will be rewarded with chest loot like nowhere else. Situated in corridors, chests can contain golden horse armour, obsidian blocks, diamonds and Nether wart, a vital ingredient in the creation of potions.

8

THE END

Well done, you've come a long way and experienced different terrains, structures and even another dimension. Your biggest test, however, is yet to come. Just finding your way there will call upon all the skills you have acquired throughout your time as an explorer. However, getting there is just one challenge ... surviving there is another story altogether.

Welcome to the End dimension.

REACHING THE END

STRONGHOLD

Finding a stronghold (see page 74) can lead you to a portal room. You can use eyes of Ender to locate a stronghold. To craft one, you will need blaze powder and an Ender pearl. They don't last long, so try to craft a good supply before beginning the search.

MEET THE MOBS

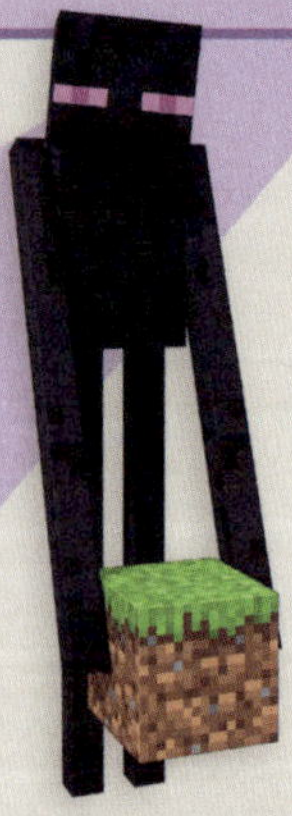

ENDERMAN

Be prepared! The clue is in the name. You will have witnessed this mob on your travels, but in the End they spawn commonly in groups of up to four. They are passive unless you look them in the eye, but if you do, they will turn hostile and run fast or even teleport to attack you.

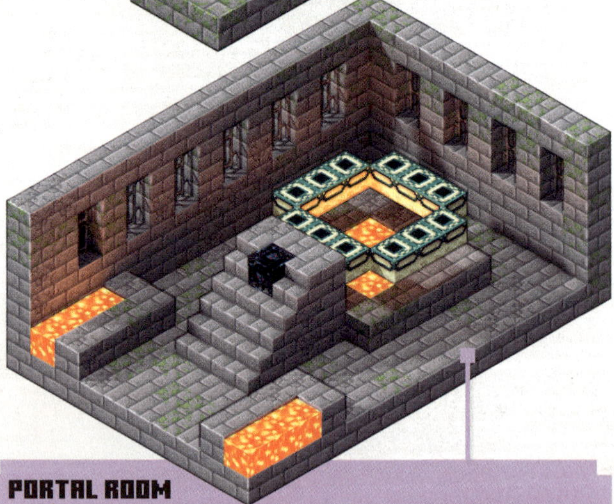

PORTAL ROOM

In a portal room, the End portal frame will be pre-existing, meaning you won't need to build one as you did with a Nether portal. In fact, End portal blocks cannot be obtained naturally and are only found in these rooms. You will, however, have to activate it.

The End is one of the most difficult places to reach in all of Minecraft. You will need to explore much of the Overworld and the Nether to find the items that will, eventually, lead you to an End portal. Reaching the End dimension is only the beginning of your biggest challenge yet, though.

ACTIVATION

Activating an End portal is a simple task. Once you have 12 eyes of Ender, crafted using blaze powder and Ender pearls, place one into each of the portal frame blocks, and the portal will activate.

END PORTAL FRAME BLOCK

EYE OF ENDER

TELEPORTATION

Once you have completed all of the necessary requirements, you will be able to use the portal to teleport to the End. Simply step into the portal block and you will travel to an obsidian platform in the End.

BIOMES:
THE END

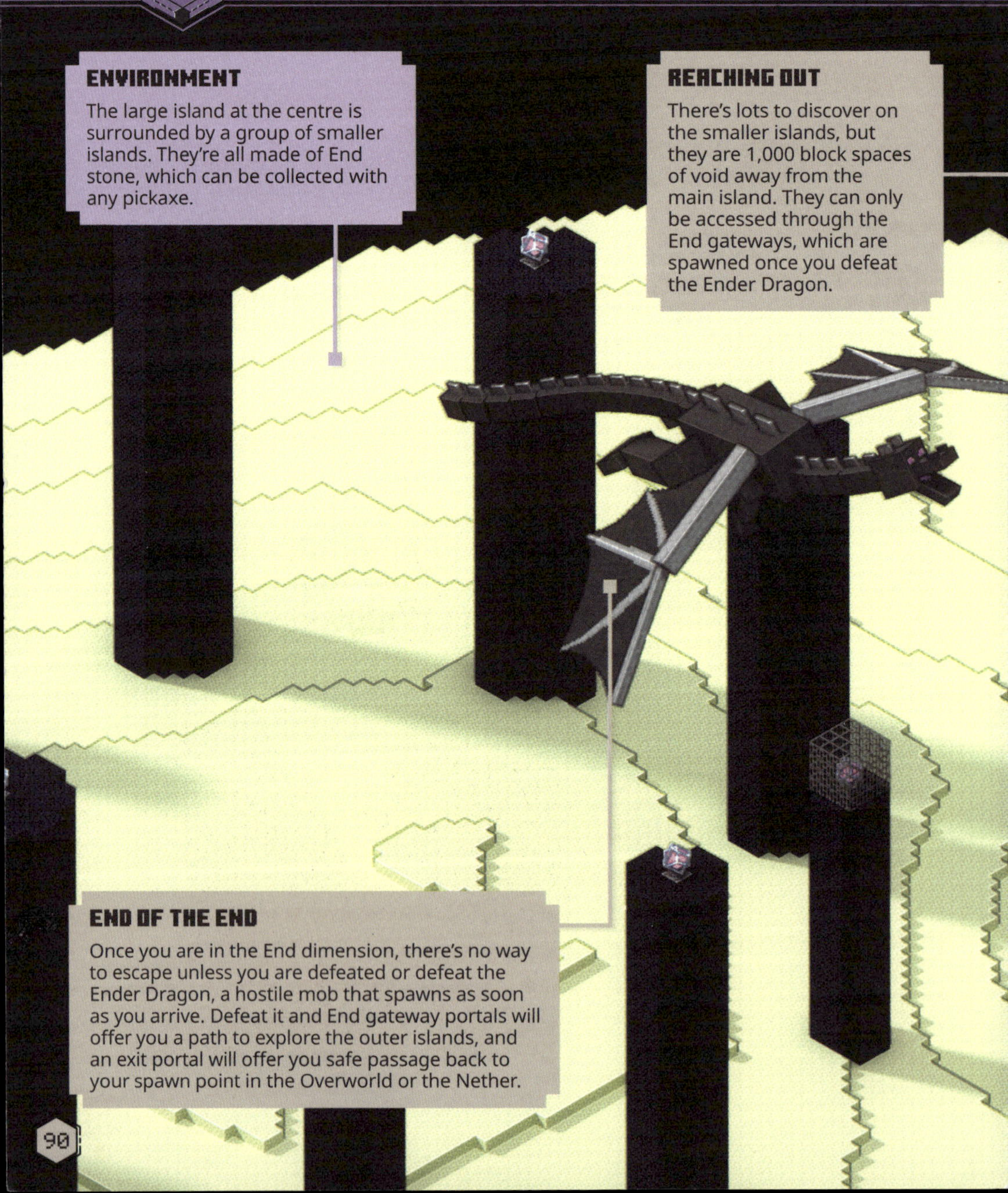

ENVIRONMENT

The large island at the centre is surrounded by a group of smaller islands. They're all made of End stone, which can be collected with any pickaxe.

REACHING OUT

There's lots to discover on the smaller islands, but they are 1,000 block spaces of void away from the main island. They can only be accessed through the End gateways, which are spawned once you defeat the Ender Dragon.

END OF THE END

Once you are in the End dimension, there's no way to escape unless you are defeated or defeat the Ender Dragon, a hostile mob that spawns as soon as you arrive. Defeat it and End gateway portals will offer you a path to explore the outer islands, and an exit portal will offer you safe passage back to your spawn point in the Overworld or the Nether.

The End is a floating environment, a dimension that is dark and spacelike. The land is made of End stone and forms islands that appear to float in the void. Only the most prepared explorers should visit here, for the encounters you will experience will be the toughest you've faced ...

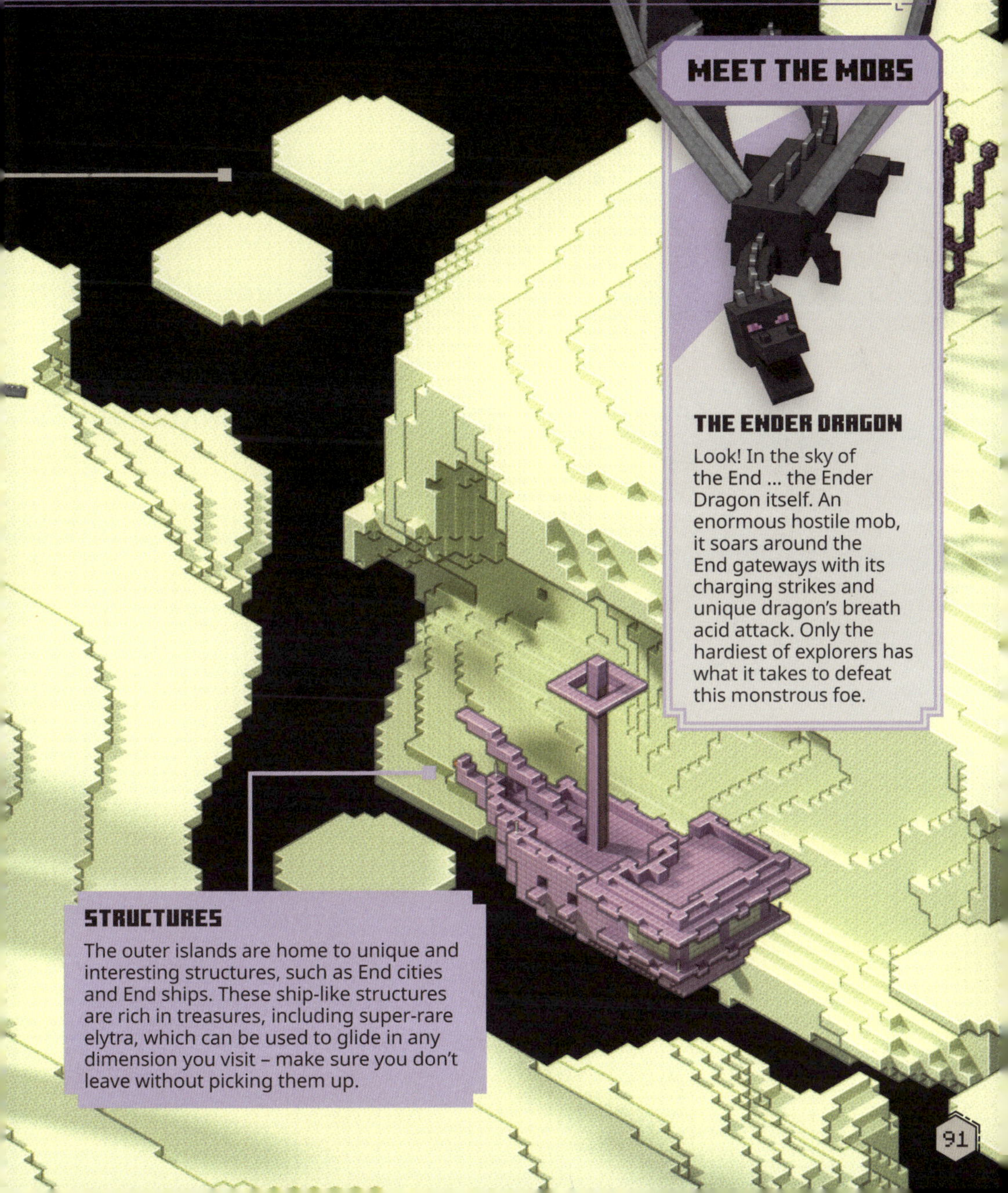

MEET THE MOBS

THE ENDER DRAGON

Look! In the sky of the End ... the Ender Dragon itself. An enormous hostile mob, it soars around the End gateways with its charging strikes and unique dragon's breath acid attack. Only the hardiest of explorers has what it takes to defeat this monstrous foe.

STRUCTURES

The outer islands are home to unique and interesting structures, such as End cities and End ships. These ship-like structures are rich in treasures, including super-rare elytra, which can be used to glide in any dimension you visit – make sure you don't leave without picking them up.

GENERATED STRUCTURES: END CITY

SMALL OR SKYSCRAPER

The city towers come in two types. Small towers are empty and contain just a few purpur slabs and a spiral staircase. Skyscrapers offer more rewards, but are home to double spiral staircases that are hard to navigate. Yet they are at least lit with End rods, a much needed light source.

Situated on the smaller islands that generate around the End's main island, End cities feature various towers made of End stone bricks and decorative purpur blocks. You can find clusters of them together in large complexes, or solo towers spaced thousands of blocks apart.

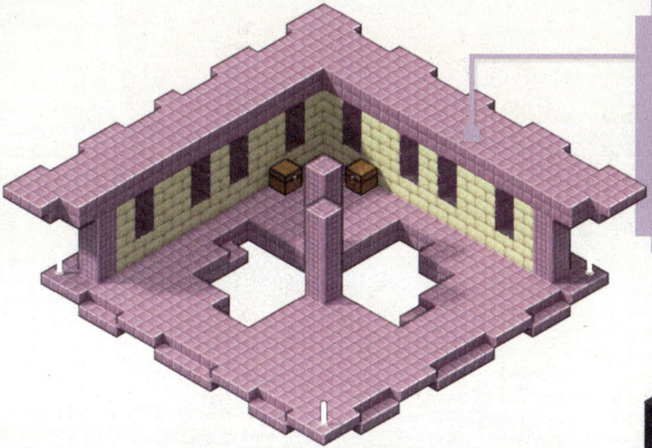

ROOMS

The many different rooms you will explore vary greatly from tower to tower. Banner rooms have unique banners hanging on the outside and a shulker on the ceiling. Loot rooms consist of two chests, and each one contains valuable loot to collect.

ENDER CHESTS

You might discover an Ender chest in an End city. These operate much in the same way as regular chests, but their contents are unique to every player – meaning your rewards are yours alone. You can access their loot from any other Ender chest you find, too.

RETURNING TO THE OVERWORLD

There's so much to explore in the End that you may never feel it's time to leave and return to the Overworld. If you do want to take all your new items back to your base, head to the Exit portal – there's much more exploring to do back in the Overworld!

GOODBYE

What a journey we've taken. We've explored all the way across the Overworld, taken a trip through the Nether and even visited the End.

There's only one thing left to do: take what you've learned and find your own path!

Where will you head? Perhaps you and a friend can seek out a camel from the desert and take it on a voyage to the ocean shores. Maybe you feel ready to approach some piglins and barter for treasures – don't forget your gold! Or maybe on your travels, you've noticed the perfect spot for a brand-new base, ready for future expeditions!

Wherever you go, there's always something new on the horizon. So keep yourself stocked up on supplies, and always stay curious.

Continue your journey with the official Minecraft Complete Handbook Collection, containing ultimate guides for Survival, Creative, Combat and Redstone, and ...

ENJOY YOUR ADVENTURES!

- MOJANG STUDIOS

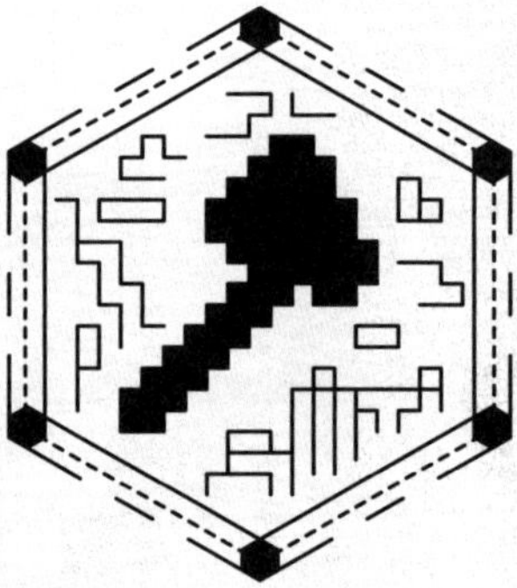